Design and Typography: Zita Group, Inc.

ISBN-978-0-9852689-1-6

Published by
The Neon Museum, Inc.
A (501)(c)(3) Non-Profit Organization
www.neonmuseum.org

Second Printing, May, 2013

This project has been financed in whole or in part with Federal funds from the National Park Service,
a division of the United States Department of the Interior,
and administered by the Nevada State Historic Preservation Office in a grant to the City of Las Vegas Historic Preservation Commission.
The contents and opinions, however, do not necessarily reflect the views or policies of the
United States Department of the Interior or the State Historic Preservation Office.

Special thanks to Brian Paco Alvarez, Las Vegas News Bureau Photo and Film Archives; Charles F. Barnard; Su Kim Chung, UNLV Library Special Collections;
Dennis McBride, Nevada State Museum, Las Vegas; Courtney Mooney, Historic Preservation Officer, City of Las Vegas;
The Neon Museum Staff and Board of Directors, and Steve Weeks, YESCO.
Additional photography by Checko Salgado.

SPECTACULAR

A History of Las Vegas Neon

Melissa Johnson, Carrie Schomig and Dorothy Wright

The Neon Museum
Las Vegas, Nevada

Dedicated to the memory of Frank Wright, Las Vegas historian, who helped to shape the Neon Museum.

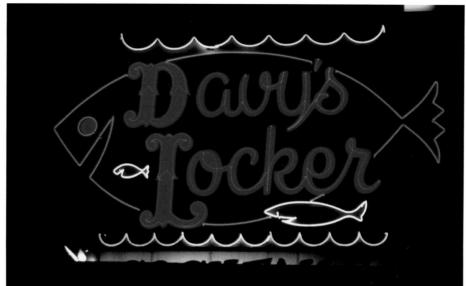

Table of Contents

Spectacular neon designs, from Fremont Street's Vegas Vic to the dazzling lights of the Strip, have been a Las Vegas trademark since the mid-20th century. Neon put the "fabulous" in "Welcome to Fabulous Las Vegas." The new light form captured the nation's imagination from the start—when neon was introduced to the United States in 1923 at Earl Anthony's Los Angeles Packard Dealership, the signs literally stopped traffic. The Golden Age of Neon exploded around the country in the 1920s and lasted through World War II. Then while neon's heyday dimmed in other parts of the nation during the 1950s, sign designers in Las Vegas began to extend their creativity to produce ever more innovative neon signs and "spectaculars" (as the largest signs were called.) Las Vegas casinos gave sign artists free rein to expand the scale and complexity of their creations. Some of the most elaborate and largest neon displays in the country came to life in Las Vegas.

Las Vegas has continually reinvented itself to keep tourists coming back. This has led to a high degree of turnover in the look of the town. Casinos have come and gone, and those that lasted usually have had numerous renovations to satisfy the public demand for novelty. In the wake of the constant refurbishment, many of the old neon signs were replaced or even lost.

Introduction

Local interest in rescuing these retired signs began in the 1970s with historic preservation groups. As early as

1978, the non-profit Preservation Association of Clark County was able to secure the Thunderbird sign, but unable to get a commitment from any local entity to place it. Then in the 1980s a committee of the Allied Arts Council began actively saving signs. Out of that the Neon Museum was born. After a partnership of several years with the City of Las Vegas, the Museum was officially incorporated as an independent, non-profit organization in 1997. Its mission was to save neon treasures and educate the public about their importance.

Since then, the Neon Museum has amassed more than 150 individual signs in its two open-air "boneyards," many donated by Young Electric Sign Company (YESCO.) Thanks to the generosity of the City of Las Vegas, land was provided to house the signs, and a temporary office for staff was donated across the street from the Neon Boneyard.

During this period the Neon Museum planned to build a large new facility which would house staff offices and smaller signs, leaving the larger ones outdoors. Fundraising proved difficult until a unique opportunity came along in 2005. The Museum agreed to save an important piece of Mid-Century Modern architecture, the La Concha Motel Lobby, to use as the Museum's Visitors' Center. Designed by acclaimed African-American architect Paul Revere Williams, the La Concha's distinctive arches were a Strip beacon since 1961. With grants from the City of Las Vegas Centennial Committee, the Nevada Commission on Cultural Affairs, the Las Vegas Convention and Visitors Authority, the Nevada Legislature, the Federal Scenic Byways Program, the City of Las Vegas, and donations from generous individuals and businesses, the building was moved six miles north from its original home next to the Riviera Hotel.

This book includes a look at these neon signs, the talented people who designed them, and their place in the history of neon in Las Vegas and in the world.

Lighting using neon. Phillip Slawinski, Wikipedia.com

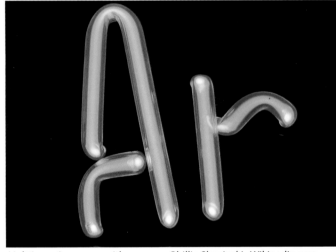

Lighting using argon with mercury. Phillip Slawinski, Wikipedia.com

A Brief
Description
of Neon Technology

There have been few technological improvements to the manufacturing and function of neon lighting since its invention in Paris in 1910. An electric discharge in neon lighting is caused by an electrode igniting an inert gas inside the tube. These inert, or noble, gases are nonflammable, colorless, and highly stable, possessing a superior degree of limited reactivity. Neon and argon are two of the six noble gases that are the easiest to obtain, and therefore they are most commonly used in neon lighting. Inert gases are attractive for the colors that they emit, but also because they produce light that is highly efficient, is cool to touch, and thus uses little energy.

To create a neon lamp, a section of narrow glass tubing is heated over a flame until it is malleable. The hot glass is then bent according to a sketched design on asbestos paper. After the tubing is bent into the desired shape and cooled, electrodes, or terminals, are inserted into the tube's open ends while the air inside the tube is partially removed through a small vent. Any residual impurities that are inside the tube are cleaned using a 30,000-volt shock of electricity, followed by a vacuum pump that removes the loosened debris. Finally, a small amount of the rare, inert gas (usually neon or argon) is drawn into the tube and the glass is permanently sealed, trapping the gas inside. An electric transformer delivers about 15,000 volts to the electrodes, which reacts with the gas inside, causing it to ionize and glow brightly and evenly along the shaft of the glass tube.

The key to neon lighting is that there is an unobstructed line of tubing between the two electrodes at the tube's ends. The maximum tubing length possible is determined by the strength of the glass tube and the capacity of the vacuum pump. Several lengths of glass may be spliced together to create a longer tube. One tube can only hold one gas but sections of the glass tubing may be tinted or coated differently to produce more than one color along the length of one tube. A well-manufactured tube can last well over 30 years.

Each of the six inert gases used in neon lighting produces its own distinctive color when electrically charged. Neon gas illuminates in a fiery orange-red color. Argon alone produces a pale lavender-blue light,

A glass bender in a sign shop. UNLV Library Special Collections.

but with a small amount of mercury added to the tube, it gives off a brilliant blue glow. Helium, krypton, radon, and xenon are prohibitively expensive inert gases and thus are less commonly used. During the high point of neon lighting production in the 1930s and 1940s, as many as 40 different colors could be produced, ranging from ruby red to midnight blue. Many of these shades are no longer available today due to lack of demand. Instead, over the past 30 years, many neon tube manufacturers have used clear glass tubing coated on the inside with phosphors that interact with the gas to produce up to 150 colors. In some cases, the exterior of the glass tubing is applied with colored enamel to produce an even broader range of hues.

Glass bending requires the knowledge of different glass properties and a skilled sense of timing. The craft can be unforgiving, as heated glass tubing must be bent within a narrow range of temperatures and once a bend is made, it cannot be redone.

Although the basic function of neon lighting has remained constant over the past century, there have been some improvements over the years. Scientists have developed lighter and smaller transformers, and high-frequency radio waves have been used to replace the electric current required by traditional methods. Nevertheless, after nearly 100 years in commercial existence, the manufacturing of neon lighting continues to be a handicraft largely produced by local electric sign shops.

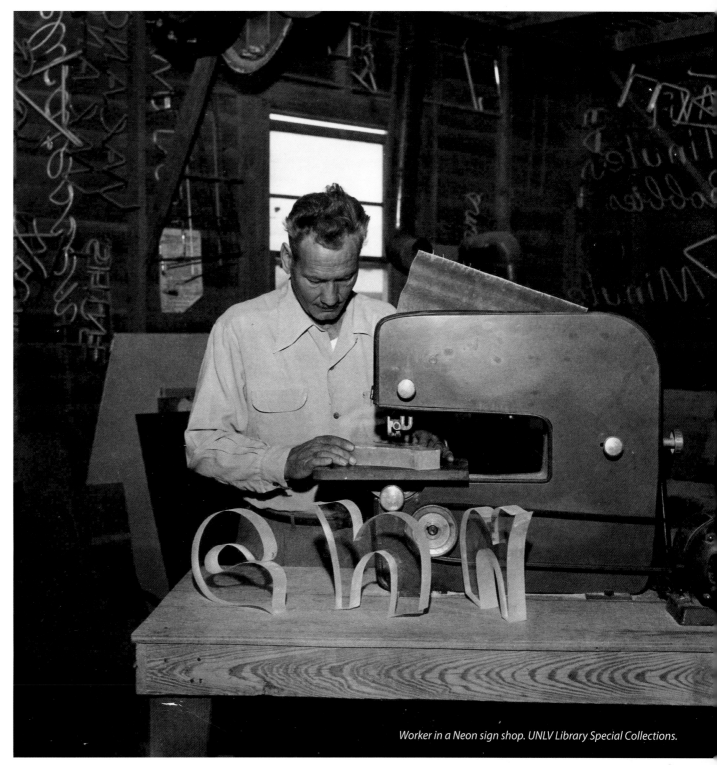

Worker in a Neon sign shop. UNLV Library Special Collections.

Georges Claude, inventor of neon.

History of Neon Lighting

The invention of neon lighting in the early 1900s was the culmination of more than 300 years of experimentation with artificial light. In the seventeenth century, physicist Evangelista Torricelli invented the glass-tube barometer, also known as "Torricelli's Tube." Torricelli later worked with Galileo Galilei (1564-1642) to experiment with mercury inserted into a glass tube vacuum during his research using the barometer. Torricelli noticed that under low pressure, the mercury contents in the tube glowed when shaken, sparking a great deal of interest within the scientific community.

Between 1700 and 1800, a handful of men experimented with vacuum-sealed glass to produce light. In 1856, Heinrich Geissler (1814-1879), a German inventor and glassmaker, came closer to producing neon lighting using a sealed low-pressure tube and running an electric current through it using electrodes. The manufacture of glass laboratory instruments became popular during the mid-nineteenth century when experiments in the natural sciences became more popular than ever. Geissler invented the Geissler Tube, which was a glass tube in which a high-voltage electric charge electrified the gas inside the tube, producing a colorful glow, depending on the type of gas used. Tests by others supported the notion that gases or vapors not only can carry an electric current, they can do it more efficiently than incandescent lights.

Interest in electricity and new methods of lighting reached technological strides in the 1890s. Inventors were able to produce light, but it burned out quickly when the gases in the tube reacted with the electrodes, quickly degrading them. In 1893, Austrian inventor Nicola Tesla created a glass-tube sign shaped into the word "LIGHT" and illuminated by phosphorescence. The sign stayed lit for only a short period of time, highlighting the fatal flaw of the technology at that time. Most of the experiments in the early 1900s involved common atmospheric gases such as nitrogen or carbon dioxide. Inventors realized that the rare, inert gases, such as xenon, neon, or argon, were less common and difficult to isolate early on, but the gases emitted brilliant colors and were highly resistant to corrosion, which was a major obstacle in the short life of the light produced from nitrogen or carbon dioxide gases. Thus, scientists focused their efforts on finding practical methods of acquiring the rare gases.

In 1907, French inventor Georges Claude (1870- 1960) became the first scientist to run an electric current through a sealed tube of neon gas, creating the first light produced with isolated neon gas. Claude went on to successfully produce neon lighting that could be commercially viable. Claude had been working to find an inexpensive way to produce large quantities of oxygen for medical uses. In his process of isolating oxygen, Claude also isolated significant quantities of leftover rare gases as by-products. He found a use for neon and argon gases by inserting each of them into glass tubes and turning on the electricity. Although argon gas was used as often as neon, the lighting method assumed the name "neon" to refer to the light produced by either gas.

In 1910, Claude's neon lamps gained public attention when he displayed his first neon sign at an automobile show in Paris' Grand Palais. Five years later, Claude invented and patented a design for a durable corrosion-resistant electrode, effectively solving the continual problem of corroding electrodes that degraded experimental neon lighting until that point. Claude acquired six U.S. patents for his neon lighting design, but his patent for the resistant electrode would prove to be his most valuable.

Although Claude viewed neon lighting as a superior alternative to everyday electric lights, the red color of the neon lamp was not a practical replacement for white incandescent light. However, neon's red glow was distinctive, and it illuminated well in the outdoors even in daylight. Claude's associate, Jacques Fonseque, saw its potential for advertising in the form of lighted signage. The malleability of glass tubing meant that it could be bent in nearly every shape for any image or message desired. For the first time, electric lights could be molded into an infinite number of shapes and letters.

Fonseque's idea for neon signage was first applied in 1912 when a Parisian barber commissioned the first commercial neon sign for his small business. The popularity of the new illuminated signs spread quickly across Paris, with as many as 160 neon signs in place by 1914. In 1919, the Paris Opera house adopted a Claude Neon marquee that used a combination of neon's red and argon's cool blue, creating a lighting that came to be called *couleur Opera*.

In 1922, a Los Angeles Packard automobile dealership owner, Earl C. Anthony, became interested in neon signs when he saw the Opera sign while visiting Paris. Anthony met with Fonseque and ordered two signs for his dealership. At a cost of $1,250 each, Fonseque produced two neon signs that spelled out "Packard" for Anthony's Packard showroom. The signs were rendered in the same vivid red-and-blue couleur Opera neon, illuminating the word "Packard" in red neon and framed by an argon-blue border.

When Anthony installed the two signs in Los Angeles in 1923, the signs literally caused a traffic-stopping sensation.

After Claude's unsuccessful attempt to sell the General Electric Company a license to his design for the patented, non-corroding electrode, the Claude Neon company began to open franchises outside of France. With an aggressive advertising campaign, Claude Neon's neon signage became popular worldwide, but nowhere to the extent that it was in the United States. In 1924, Claude personally set up his first American franchise in New York City. For others, a Claude Neon franchise could be purchased for the sum of $100,000 in cash, which gave the buyer use of the patented neon sign design and an inexpensive supply of neon and argon gas. Despite

Neon used for cove lighting on the interior of the Earl Carroll Theater in Los Angeles, as seen in 1938.
Los Angeles Public Library Photo Collection.

A neon sign created for the Mobil Oil Company, featuring its well-known Pegasus logo. UNLV Library Special Collections.

the princely down payment required, Claude Neon franchises emerged across the nation due to the burgeoning popularity of neon signs, but also due in part to the fact that neon glass tubing was fragile and did not ship well without breakage, making local, small-scale neon manufacturing shops a necessity in most cities. After Claude Neon's initial launch in the United States, the company's franchises soon cropped up across Europe, Latin America, China, Japan, and Australia.

Neon signage and advertisements were quickly adapted by nationally based franchises and local businesses alike. Established national companies such as American Radiator, Standard Oil, and Lucky Strike cigarettes were among the first to commission neon signs. Neon's success skyrocketed through the Jazz Age of the late 1920s and even through the stock market crash of 1929—the year when sales at Claude Neon increased by a record 40 percent over the previous year. Although bootlegged neon signs were common when Claude Neon still held the patents, the company continued to produce the vast majority of neon lighting manufactured. Claude Neon's patented neon electrode design eventually expired in 1932, opening the way for the proliferation of legitimate competition. Independent neon shops sprang into business quickly thereafter, and by 1939, there were an estimated 2,000 neon sign companies operating in the United States.

Neon signs had become an unparalleled medium for advertising by the 1930s. The neon sign uniquely communicated to the automobile traveler, who was becoming increasingly common in the American landscape throughout the 1920s and 1930s. As cities and the countryside became transformed into a network of roadways and highways, roadside signage evolved into a more visually aggressive medium in an effort to capture the attention of the fast-moving viewer. As a result, the brightly lit neon sign became a popular mode of advertisement and an icon for roadway culture and the new, modern changes of the twentieth century.

Downtown business districts in cities nationwide

Las Vegas' former 5th St. Liquor Store's animated signage, created in 1946. The sign has been restored by The Neon Museum and is currently on exhibit on Casino Center Blvd.

gases and tube coatings. Intricately detailed images could be rendered in complex arrangements of bent-glass tubing. The most successful designs went beyond capturing the attention of the advertiser's audience, and strove to amuse, surprise, and delight.

Some of the most elaborate neon signs created an illusion of animation by lighting separate tubes in sequence. The first automatic equipment for these "moving" images was produced in 1932 by Time-O-Matic. By adapting existing technology from flashers that had been previously used for incandescent lighting, neon lights could be set to pause and repeat to create the appearance of animated movement, such as a moving car or a waving hand. Common images achieved were running horses, walking bakers, dripping faucets for plumbing shops, or a beverage pouring into a glass. Neon animation reached its height in America in New York City's Times Square and, later, in the entertainment districts of Las Vegas. Times Square began its transition to spectacular neon signage by the 1930s with dazzling, brightly lit signs adorning the multi-storied facades of the buildings.

Early neon was also uniquely suited for architectural decoration. Buildings in New York and Chicago used neon tubing to outline distinctive architectural features, transforming the buildings themselves into a backdrop for attention grabbing advertising. Even some churches used neon to draw attention to the buildings and their religious symbols. In 1928, one person counted more than 60 neon-outlined crucifixes within Midtown Manhattan alone.

Neon was particularly well-suited for Art Deco and Streamline Moderne architectural motifs. Like the styles themselves, neon's steady glow symbolized modernity, progress, and vitality. Thin tubes of neon could easily outline the curved, streamlined edges

and portholes of the Streamline Moderne style. The light reflected well on Art Deco's glossy and metallic surfaces. For a more subdued effect, concealed neon tubes incorporated into soffits and coves created indirect, ambient lighting along ceiling edges. Neon also became fashionable for commercial interior lighting in the 1930s. A typical movie palace might display a flamboyant, multicolor neon marquee over the entrance and carry the same motif into the lobby with more dazzling neon light to decorate the interior walls and soffits. Past the lobby, neon was often employed for more practical use along theater aisles to guide movie goers to their seats.

Produced by skilled craftsmen, neon became an art form. Neon fabrication was a hand-crafted process that allowed for a wide range of individuality by the fabricator. Very little neon was mass-produced, and this was limited to small products such as clocks and beer signs, a practice that continues today. While large sign companies might have employed a neon designer, self-trained employees of small businesses often drew sketches for their signs themselves. The sign designs for modest mom-and-pop shops were sometimes surprisingly intricate. Many larger companies, such as Coca- Cola, ordered the fabrication of large quantities of neon signs and gave them away as a promotional tool to businesses that sold their products.

In the 1930s and 1940s, neon signage was available to all types of businesses because it was relatively inexpensive. Competition between sign companies kept the cost of neon fabrication low. Trade schools in Philadelphia and New York supplied the market with large numbers of professional neon glass benders, sustaining a highly competitive market for neon manufacturing jobs.

Neon sign design generally continued to follow the

also began to glow in neon during the 1930s. Hotels, restaurants and bars, auto dealerships, bakeries, cleaners, grocers, and virtually every other type of commercial establishment embraced the new signage, and often with creative flair. Meanwhile, competition spurred more technologically innovative sign design. One sign could employ a variety of colors using different

YESCO workers taking the Silver Slipper shoe from the YESCO shop to the site of the new hotel-casino. UNLV Special Collections.

Four Mile Bar, Nevada State Museum.

pre-war styles during the years immediately following the war. However, by the end of the 1940s, the zig-zag Art Deco and Streamline Moderne styles began to fade as more mid-century Modern motifs gained favor. The newer styles were plainer and lacked ornamentation and exaggerated architectural features.

Technological advances in new materials during the World War II era had a profound effect on neon signage. Industrially manufactured building materials, such as concrete, ceramic tile, steel, and plate glass gained widespread use for purposes of both style and economy for a wide range of building types. While neon signs were almost exclusively made from sheet metal through the 1940s, plastics became available by 1950 and the new material gave birth to a

new generation of signage. In the 1950s, sign companies manufactured light boxes made from Plexiglass-fronted shadow boxes that were back-lighted by fluorescent lighting. Signs made from plastic materials became a cheaper advertising medium than neon. Meanwhile, signs with exposed neon tubing came to be derided as old-fashioned and demand for them waned. As a result, neon lighting began its steady decline in the 1950s.

The nationwide downward trend of neon sign manufacturing continued into the 1960s and 1970s. With the loss of favor, most of the neon manufacturing shops from the 1930s and 1940s had closed by 1970. As a consequence to the industry, the availability of materials, such as the rarest gases and colored glass tubing, all but disappeared.

Popular taste had also changed by the 1980s as more subdued, conservative versions of Modern styles took precedence over the flamboyant and colorful styles of the 1950s and 1960s. Natural materials and colors were emphasized with greater frequency, and signs became smaller. The preference for the light box using internal florescent lighting with plastic fronts continued, while neon was manufactured as more of a novelty or to create a kitschy, retrospective aesthetic.

By the late 1980s, the 2,000 neon plants that operated at the end of the 1930s had dwindled to around 250 shops. During the heyday of neon sign design in the 1930s and early 1940s, most of the companies that produced neon signs employed at least one neon designer. During the last half of the twentieth century, skilled workers and craftsmen of neon lighting became a rarity, a trend that continues into the present day.

While neon technology has remained largely static over the past 100 years, sign design has continually evolved, replacing neon with the latest state-of-the-art technology. The current use of fiber-optic video screens and microcomputers is increasingly edging out the use of neon lighting. Nevertheless, neon still survives in new commercial signage and as an art form, keeping the few remaining neon sign manufacturers in operation.

Neon lighting in Las Vegas has followed a different historical path than the rest of the country. The city's desert landscape and its emphasis on tourism have provided a backdrop that has been exceptionally conducive to neon. As demand for neon signage began to wane nationwide in the 1950s, in Las Vegas neon began to realize greater heights of grandeur than had ever been attempted. Since then, neon has been a vital element of the city's image and has thrived better there than anywhere else in the United States.

Las Vegas, circa 1906. UNLV Library Special Collections.

"Nowhere is light used so fully as a means of defining space… almost every piece of architecture plays the role of stage set, to make us think of other places… and in Las Vegas these other places are palaces and fantasy castles… Xanadu!"

— Architectural critic Paul Goldberger ("A Knockout First Look at Las Vegas," The New York Times. April 23, 1978).

History of Neon Signs in Las Vegas

Early Las Vegas

Las Vegas began as a railroad division point in 1905, when Montana Senator William Clark's San Pedro, Los Angeles and Salt Lake Railroad auctioned off lots to create a new town. The verdant oasis called Las Vegas (in Spanish, "the meadows") was fed by underground springs that had supported a few ranches in the area as well as small roaming bands of Paiutes. Previous to the railroad coming, the earliest non-native settlement was the Mormon Mission, established in 1855, as a way station on the California trail. It lasted only two years, when the climate and other challenges took their toll on the missionaries, who returned to Salt Lake City. Eventually the property was developed as a ranch, ending up under the ownership of Helen Stewart. The ranch fed travelers and miners in the area until 1902, when Stewart sold most of her property and water rights to the railroad.

The little town took shape quickly, with concrete and wood frame buildings soon replacing tent structures. The hardy souls who defied the blistering heat stayed to create a community, which slowly acquired the trappings of civilization. In 1909 the Nevada Legislature carved Clark County, named for the Montana Senator, out of the southern half of Lincoln County, so residents would not have to make the 175 mile wagon trip to Pioche, the Lincoln County seat. Las Vegas, population 947, edged then-booming Searchlight for the honor of the new Clark County seat. In 1911, Las Vegas was incorporated as a city.

Las Vegas grew slowly after 1911, content to be a railroad stop, with most jobs linked to the railroad machine shops or to hotels and restaurants that served travelers. Enterprising souls who wished to develop land outside of Clark's Las Vegas Townsite had to contend with the railroad's subsidiary, the Las Vegas Land and Water Company, which tightly controlled the water and sewage system. Fremont Street was the main artery, leading from the Spanish-style railroad depot where the Plaza Hotel now stands. Stores, hotels, restaurants and businesses lined the street.

Further east on Fourth Street, the town's elite built comfortable bungalow-style homes. Elsewhere in the townsite were churches, a school and a small hospital. Saloons were restricted to Block 16 of the forty-block townsite. Block 16 also housed illegal brothels which were tolerated by the authorities until World War II.

The first signs in Las Vegas were banners hung from tent structures. When permanent buildings replaced tents, signs were simple hand-painted letters on wood, sometimes placed directly on the building façade

or the side of the building. In 1906 when electricity became available, the signs were sometimes lit by an overhead incandescent bulb. Other signs relied on the newly erected street lights for illumination. Occasionally a metal sign would project perpendicular to a store-front, or be supported by a metal pipe or a wooden pole. After 1920, signs grew more sophisticated, with an occasional animated border of lamps that "chased" with manually operated switches.

The town's dependence on the railroad took a

Fremont Street 1926. UNLV Special Collections

Fremont Street late 1930s. UNLV Library Special Collections.

downward turn when Las Vegas joined a nationwide railroad strike that grew violent. In retaliation the railroad (by then the Union Pacific) moved its vast machine repair shops north to Caliente. Many workers lost their jobs and Las Vegas went into a slump. It was not until later in the 1920s that the town's prospects began looking up with the announcement of a massive federal dam construction project to tame the Colorado River, thirty miles from Las Vegas. People flocked to Las Vegas looking for work even before construction began in 1931. While the rest of the nation suffered the effects of the Great Depression, in Las Vegas the population more than doubled to 5,165 from 1920's count of 2,304. The influx of workers brought jobs and customers for Las Vegas stores, saloons, and service providers.

Neon began glowing on Fremont Street about the time the Boulder Dam Act was announced in 1928. On September 28, 1928, the Las Vegas Review reported, "The Overland Hotel is displaying a new Neon gas-electric sign, of the most modern design, adding considerably to the appearance of that section of the city." The Overland was, if not the first, certainly one of the first neon signs in Las Vegas. Not long after, in April 1929, the Las Vegas Neon Electric Sign Company opened for business and began building neon signs. On April 30, 1929 the Las Vegas Age reported that the Golden Hotel was sporting a new neon sign, which "was one of the finest in Las Vegas," courtesy of Las Vegas Neon Sign Company. On August 13, 1929 the Las Vegas Neon Sign Company announced it had moved to a larger space "due to their many new

contracts." They reported working on a "big new sign" for the Northern Club. By 1930 the company had completed neon signs for the Gateway Hotel, Beckley's Clothing Store and the Mission Cigar Store.

Las Vegas civic leaders knew that the Dam construction would provide only a temporary boost to the town's economy. They needed a new industry, one that would last. Tourism was the answer. In 1931, in response to the ravages of the Great Depression, the Nevada legislature liberalized Nevada's gaming laws, which already allowed for card games and slot machines, although forbidding cash prizes. In 1931, table games were legalized. The other ace in the hole was divorce—liberalized to a six-week waiting period, also in 1931. Together with already lax marriage laws that required no waiting period and no blood tests, gambling and divorce were to form the bedrock of the early tourism industry. In 1933, with the repeal of the Volstead Act which had established Prohibition against alcohol, Las Vegas was poised to receive visitors with open arms and flowing liquor.

1930s

Improved roadways aided the influx of travelers. Boulder Highway, constructed to provide materials and support to the Dam project, fed into Fremont Street, bringing dam workers and Arizona visitors to Las Vegas. Highway 91 (inside the city limits known as Fifth Street, later Las Vegas Blvd.) became a major route, and some far-sighted entrepreneurs built nightclubs to take advantage of it. The Pair O'Dice, owned by Al Capone's friend Frank Detra, was one of the first clubs to be built on the L.A. highway. California gambler Guy McAfee later bought the property and re-named it the 91 Club. McAfee is often credited with bestowing "The Strip" moniker on Highway 91. McAfee sold the property to R.E. Griffith, who built the Last Frontier.

Hoover Dam. Nevada State Museum

of businesses on the city's downtown Fremont Street. The signs were similar to those in other American towns at the time. They were enameled cabinets made from sheet metal and were either one-sided and attached to the building façade, or were double-faced and mounted on one end like a flag if the building was in an urban setting or upon a pole at a roadside outside of town. For lettering, popular fonts were plain, sans-serif block lettering or "western" motifs with stylized serif lettering. Although neon quickly became popular during the 1930s, its use was not wide spread at that time. Businesses that could not afford the expense of neon still used hand-painted metal signs, some of which were lighted by incandescent light bulbs mounted on goose-neck reflectors. Other businesses simply advertised with painted awnings.

Three different forms of electric signage would emerge in Las Vegas over the next 30 years. The first was the two-dimensional sign attached to a building façade.

These were common along Fremont Street, where narrow buildings were located side-by-side and a building's façade was the only place for businesses to place their signage. The second sign type was the free-standing sign attached to a tall pylon, also known as the superpylon. The pylon sign was visible from long distances and became more common along the Las Vegas Boulevard to cater to highway travelers south of the city center. The third and last sign type to evolve in Las Vegas was the lighted porte-cochere in which a street-facing building extended its automobile canopy to the street in a dramatic and oversized lighted display.

In March 1932, the Apache Hotel, where Binion's stands today, opened as the most luxurious hotel in Las Vegas at that time. Designed by local architect A. Lacy Worswick, the hotel had 100 rooms and even included an elevator to the third floor, which was unprecedented in the city. The building incorporated Native American-inspired zig-zag motifs on the interior

Another new kind of business that appeared along Highway 91 and Boulder Highway was the motel, sometimes called in the early days "autel" or "auto court." Usually free-standing cabins at first, the motels catered to the automobile traveler and families, providing cheap, accessible accommodations. By the early 1930s there were auto courts on the main arteries, Highway 91, Fremont Street and Boulder Highway. One of the first was the Gateway Motel, built in 1930 on the corner of Charleston and Fifth Street. The Gateway, with Spanish style cabins, still stands. Its neon sign, date unknown, is one of the earliest still in its original location. The Normandie Motel, built 1937 by Bob Huffey. Betty Willis, who designed the Welcome to Las Vegas sign, created the Normandie sign in the 1950s.

During the 1930s, early neon commercial signs in Las Vegas were typically attached to the front façade

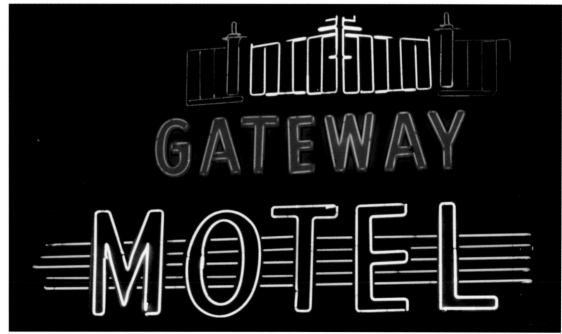
Gateway Motel. Nevada State Museum.

of the building's arches. The bar at the ground floor, called the Apache bar, was considered to be the most sophisticated in the town. The Apache Hotel also included a gaming hall that used a vertical, building-fronted neon sign that announced the hotel's name, "Apache," to the streetfront. By the early 1930s, neon was being used for everyday commercial buildings in the country's largest cities. However, although the Apache Hotel was a leading edge in style and design in Las Vegas, the full application of neon on a large scale in the town would not fully take root for another 20 years.

Several sign companies operated in Las Vegas in the 1930s. The Las Vegas Neon Electric Sign Company was one of the busiest. The American Sign Co. sign shop also produced signs during this period, but it is unclear if they produced signs lighted with neon. Other early companies were the Nevada Neon Sign Co., F.G. Keyes, and others outside of Las Vegas. However, the Young Electric Sign Company (YESCO) was the neon company that went on to make the biggest impact in Las Vegas in the twentieth century.

Years before the conception of YESCO, sign designer Thomas Young opened the Thomas Young Sign Co. commercial sign company in Ogden, Utah, in 1920. Young had received both informal and formal training in sign painting and fabrication and had found employment at sign manufacturing companies in Ogden until starting his own business. By 1927, Young's employed 27 full-time employees and kept a brisk business throughout the intermountain region. Young looked to expand with branch offices to the west. After first establishing a YESCO shop in Salt Lake City, he entered Nevada to extend his business to Las Vegas, where he arrived in 1932. Around this time, YESCO had also become the first company in the region to manufacture its own glass neon tubing.

Valley Motel, East Fremont. Nevada State Museum.

Operating from a hotel room at the newly opened Apache Hotel on Fremont Street, Young started his Las Vegas business by becoming the sole licensee and manufacturer of the California-based company Q.R.S., or Quick Reliable Signs. In 1936, The Thomas Young Sign Company was renamed the Young Electric Sign Company, shortened YESCO. YESCO would eventually establish a Las Vegas manufacturing plant in 1945, but even before then the company would produce many of the earliest iconic neon signs along Fremont Street.

Many of YESCO's contracts for the signs it manufactured were lease agreements that included service contracts for the life of the lease. When the lessee eventually removed the sign, the contract stipulated that it returned to YESCO, which either recycled the sign's parts or retired the sign to a designated boneyard lot at the outskirts of Las Vegas. YESCO had several boneyards over the years, but the boneyard from the 1970s and the old neon signs that accumulated there would eventually be donated to The Neon Museum of Las Vegas in 1996.

Early advertisement.
Courtesy of YESCO

Meanwhile, the federal government completed the Boulder Dam Project in1935 with the opening of Hoover Dam. The dam produced a surplus of electricity and water that were channeled to Las Vegas, fueling the town's growth and its ability to thrive in its arid, remote desert location. However, residents began to see the erosion of the population of dam construction workers and the economic stability they provided over the previous five years. Residents began to worry about the city's economy. The captive audience of construction workers who supported local businesses began to move away. The most high-profile gaming club in the Las Vegas Valley, The Meadows, closed, and seemed to foreshadow an uncertain future. The loss of traffic between Boulder City and Las Vegas indicated that Las Vegas might return to its existence as a small, struggling railroad town.

Well before 1935, Las Vegans began to look elsewhere to keep people coming to their city. Local boosters decided to use the old west as a new promotional tool. This practice would last for the following three decades. In 1934, in an effort to promote Las Vegas' image as an old frontier town, the local Elks Clubs began planning an annual western festival and a rodeo called "Helldorado." The town bought into the idea, and the following year, Helldorado Village appeared, replete with wood-plank sidewalks, and western-style street features such as hitching posts and watering troughs. The tourism ploy was successful and became an annual event in the city.

The promotion of the "Old Western" theme was also used by many of the early Las Vegas casinos in their illuminated signage. In 1936, Las Vegas' western-themed Boulder Club hired YESCO to redesign its 1933 sign. Located on Fremont Street, the new sign combined a tall, vertical, double-sided "blade" sign that read "Boulder Club" in vertical lettering above a wedge-shaped marquee scripted with "Enjoy the Old West," and a subscript, "Craps-Faro Bank-Bar- Cocktail Lounge" on both sides of the marquee. A six foot neon clock was added to the bottom which the *Review Journal* said "would be known as the town clock." In 1946, YESCO would add a large sign component next to the

Helldorado mid-1930s. UNLV Library Special Collections.

Another common early sign type was the horizontally oriented, V-shaped or wedge-shaped marquee that was attached to the building façade above its ground-story entrance. Smaller businesses used signs that simply announced their product, such as "café," "saloon," or "liquors." In addition to the lettering, any sign might be framed in incandescent bulbs or outlined in neon tubing to make them brighter and give them visual presence. The Las Vegas Club, which opened in 1931, and the 1929 Boulder club, were two of the earliest to use neon-lighted signage on Fremont Street in Downtown Las Vegas after the 1928 Overland Hotel.

Between 1935 and 1945, themes of the "Old West" dominated all tourism campaigns in Las Vegas. Many other western towns advertised the same allure, but Las Vegas was popularly noted for its flamboyant publicity campaign that used the theme of the "Last Frontier" in the American West. The city's adopted slogan was "Still a Frontier Town," and local residents reinforced it by continuing to ride horses through town, and by wearing western-style clothing. Residents considered many of Las Vegas' attributes part of its western character. This included the state's convenient marriage and divorce laws, low taxes, plentiful alcohol, rodeos, and most of all, all-night gambling. At the same time, residents promoted its proximity to Hoover Dam, calling Las Vegas the "Gateway to World's Greatest Engineering Project." While the western theme would appeal to Americans from the nation's eastern regions, boosters had hoped that Hoover Dam would also attract tourists from western states as well.

Although the tourism campaign did boost visitation to Las Vegas by 1939, the economy was not as robust as it had been during the economic bonanza of the Hoover Dam construction. Local Las Vegans' initial reluctance to fully promote gambling might have initially hurt tourism

vertical sign that read "Boulder Club: Bets from a Dime Up" in large lettering that was attached to an open, metal scaffolding that stood high over the roof of the building YESCO's illuminated collage of the three signs for the Boulder Club was larger than any other sign on Fremont Street and it became the first spectacular display of neon signage in Las Vegas.

Many gambling halls' façades along Fremont Street had become illuminated with neon lights by the late 1930s. The signs in downtown Las Vegas were limited to the depth of the sidewalks, which were extended between 10 and 14 feet wide. This limitation forced signs to grow vertically in size, often in the form of a hanging sign attached to the building front, and featuring stacked (vertical) lettering. Supported by metal framing and bracket supports, the vertical signs allowed signage to become taller and larger than ever before.

to the city. At that time, there were still no luxury resorts established in the valley, and many visitors were repelled by the notion of "roughing it" in a frontier town. As a result, tourists spent little money and did not stay long. Many visitors did not find the city attractive, including Secretary of Interior Harold Ickes, who unflatteringly referred to it as "an ugly little town". Las Vegas persisted as a stop on the way to more important places.

1940s

The city's fears of stagnant growth were short-lived, and by the 1940s, Las Vegas experienced its second economic boom during the World War II years. Las Vegas' tourism surged and the city's popularity among tourists began to surpass that of Hoover Dam. The relaxed atmosphere of Las Vegas might have also appealed to tourists for relief during wartime rationing. In the federally-sponsored effort to ration materials and supplies, commercial industries ceased and were replaced by World War II war-manufacturing activities centered on defense plants and installations. Las Vegas benefited from federal resources invested in nearby military plants, such as the Basic Magnesium Plant to the south, which opened in 1942, and the Las Vegas Army Air Corps Gunnery School north of the city, which opened in 1941. While businesses in town kept pace with pre-war levels during this time, neon sign production all but stopped from the prohibition of the use of sheet metal during the war years. Since most neon signs were constructed of neon lighting attached to sheet-metal cabinets, the short supply of commercially available metal stalled neon sign shop activity.

The transformation of Las Vegas from a small regional railroad distribution center into a tourist and recreation center in the Southwest was evident by 1940. By this time, the town encompassed 12 square miles,

with public buildings, businesses, and residences that were established or under construction within this area. All of the casinos and businesses were located within the 40-block townsite near the Union Pacific Railroad depot. Fremont Street became the center of nightlife, with the longest-established casinos and other businesses operating there since the 1930s.

Las Vegas began to fully embrace neon in the 1940s. From the brilliant effect of neon lighting, Fremont Street was later nicknamed the Glitter Gulch. Neon lit up the casinos, restaurants, hotels, drugstores, and saloons. Most of the last residences were pushed out of Fremont Street's downtown area by 1940, replaced by new hotels, restaurants, and more gambling clubs. Many of these establishments were in close proximity to the train depot for the convenience of railroad passengers. This became especially important when the gasoline shortage increased the number of railway passengers during World War II.

The decades-long competition for larger and more flamboyant signs on Las Vegas' Fremont Street unofficially began in the 1940s. As new casinos in the commercial district gained flashier neon signs, so did the neighboring competition. While many buildings in Las Vegas employed permanent sidewalk canopies as early as 1905, in the early 1940s, when neon became common nationwide, the buildings' front canopies become larger and wider to support the growing size of the neon signs. In effect, the signs created marquees at the front of buildings. Most of the businesses along Fremont Street had a glowing neon sign, lighting the downtown blocks in a multi-color display at night. In comparison with downtown's Fremont Street, the El Rancho Vegas and the Last Frontier casinos along the Los Angeles Highway south of the city appeared dim with their relatively small signs glowing in the distant darkness.

The El Rancho's roadside signage across the street. UNLV Library Special Collections.

In 1941, the 59-room El Cortez hotel and casino opened in Las Vegas' downtown Fremont Street area. The establishment was larger than the existing casinos, and, unlike the modified storefronts, was entirely new construction with a one-story arcade along the side facade. In a Spanish-revival style, the façade was faced with bricks with weeping mortar and the roof was red tile while a large metal sign announced the casino club's name. The El Cortez gradually built up more signage across the canopy at the building's first story and added a tall blade sign with an arrow positioned over the door.

23

The El Cortez.
UNLV Library Special Collections.

The El Rancho resort, located south of city limits. UNLV Library Special Collections.

Located at the corner of Fremont and First streets, the Pioneer Club opened in 1942 as another western-themed casino. The casino utilized an existing three-story brick building and added neon lighting across the façade. A large, vertical neon sign with Old Western typeface announced the club, along with stylized images of a miner, a mule, and a Conestoga wagon.

The resort industry began in 1941 with the opening of the El Rancho Vegas, the first resort hotel to be located south of the city boundaries along the Los Angeles Highway. Los Angeles casino operator Thomas Hull, an experienced hotel owner who operated other El Rancho hotels in major California cities, opened El Rancho Vegas. Hull decided to bypass the downtown district of the city, and instead located his casino in a resort-style complex outside of the city limits where the taxes were lower, land was cheaper, and water rights were easier to obtain. The site encompassed 133 acres along the Los Angeles Highway (now Las Vegas Boulevard) at San Francisco Street (now Sahara Avenue.)

Designed by architect Wayne McAllister, El Rancho Vegas established a benchmark south of the city by introducing the concept of the fantasy theme to casinos and also establishing the motel building form along the Strip. The central building at El Rancho Vegas was painted white and topped by a windmill tower outlined in orange neon. The tower served as a beacon for travelers driving along the highway south of the city. The windmill featured neon letters that read, "El Rancho Vegas". Although the El Rancho recycled the Old Western themes already established among the older clubs and casinos in downtown Las Vegas, Hull enlivened the resort's entertainment by importing experienced dancing showgirls from California.

The Last Frontier, another resort hotel located south of the city limits, opened in October 1942. Both the Last Frontier and El Rancho Vegas would exemplify the combined image of luxury and the old west as popular tourist attractions during the early 1940s. By 1947, Hull's El Rancho would establish the pattern of large highway motels and casinos located just south of the city limit. Ultimately, the precedent set by El Rancho was more influential than Benjamin Siegel's famous Flamingo hotel and casino that opened almost six years after El Rancho in 1946.

The Thunderbird, showing a second bird that was added later in 1965. UNLV Library Special Collections.

The population of Las Vegas swelled and the city grew exponentially as its original townsite continued to fill in and expand after 1945. The gambling industry significantly contributed to the growth of the city. The casinos brought identity to the town's downtown core, but the housing built in the 1950s consisted of subdivisions that began to decentralize the city.

During this time, Las Vegas began to figure prominently in the cultural mindset of Southern California and Los Angeles, the city to which Las Vegas had been physically and culturally tied

since the two cities were connected by the SPLA&SL Railroad in 1905. Although Las Vegas' tourism was centered more on the entertainment industry than Los Angeles' larger and more diverse economy, the difference between the two regions was that, in Las Vegas, the leisure lifestyle flowed non-stop, in the 24-hour casinos, clubs, and restaurants. Las Vegas' "anything-goes" attitude became the country's experimental playground. To compete with each other, hotels, casinos, and resorts worked hard to offer any amenity and to attract more celebrities.

After 1945, casino gambling became the centerpiece of the city's tourism enterprise as Las Vegans began to fully realize the economic potential for casinos in the city. Although businesses south of the city began to rely less on promoting the "Old West" theme to attract tourists, the city's Chamber of Commerce decided to name the three block strip along Fremont Street "Glitter Gulch," to draw attention to the dense lighted display of casinos and clubs.

The Flamingo opened on Christmas Eve 1946 as the third casino on the Strip. Eschewing Old Western themes of the El Rancho and El Cortez, the Flamingo's early proprietor, the infamous mobster Bugsy Siegel, set a formal dress code for both staff and the patrons.

Two years later, the Thunderbird casino-hotel became the fourth casino resort to open on the Strip. It was designed in a sophisticated style that rivaled the Modern Californian-born style of its neighbor, The Flamingo. Its architecture conceived the style with its wide, low-pitched gable roof that was supported by simple, unadorned columns. It also included the first porte-cochere (an automobile canopy at the entrance) on the Strip. The Thunderbird's crowning element was a tower with a three-dimensional bird in cubist form perched with its talons born into the roof. The sharp edges of the bird and its outstretched wings were outlined in neon. A second neon-lighted bird stood atop the pole sign on the front lawn by the highway. The Thunderbird's sign was designed by the Graham Neon Sign Company and consisted of several displays of façade-mounted neon lettering. As was typical in 1948 on The Strip, the Thunderbird's signs did not overwhelm the architecture, but were decorative complements to it.

The Golden Nugget also opened in 1946, located in Glitter Gulch at the corner of Fremont and Second streets. The new sign broadly displayed its name and the year "1905" to pay homage the beginnings of Las Vegas, rather than to the casino itself. YESCO designed the first of the Golden Nugget's neon-and-metal signs that became progressively larger over the following decade. In 1950, a 48 x 48-foot sign holding even larger lettering displaying the Golden Nugget surmounted the existing signage, dwarfing the one-story building below it.

The Pioneer Club shortly after the addition of Vegas Vic, installed in 1951. Still in place, the sign has become one of YESCO's most popular and recognizable works. UNLV Library Special Collections.

By the end of World War II, YESCO had built up an impressive portfolio, including signs for The Golden Nugget, The Las Vegas Club, The Eldorado Club, El Rancho, and The Pioneer Club among many other gaming clubs throughout town. YESCO had more than adequately established its presence and opened its Las Vegas neon manufacturing shop to ride the wave of prosperity that carried the city into the 1950s.

Across the street from the Golden Nugget, The Eldorado casino, on the first floor of the Apache Hotel, also boasted a large canopy sign whose cursive script swept across the second level of its façades on Fremont and Second streets, joined by a corner piece between the two halves. The Eldorado Club laid claim to the largest neon sign in the city at the time. While the casinos on the Strip aimed to attract celebrities and big-headline performances, the casinos of Fremont Street operated on a different scale, specializing in slot machine gaming. The Eldorado was later bought by Texan Benny Binion in 1951 and renamed The

The Horseshoe, pictured in the early 1950s.
UNLV Library Special Collections.

Fremont Street, early 1950s. UNLV Library Special Collections.

Horseshoe (and later renamed Binion's Horseshoe, and currently Binion's.) The Eldorado's sign was then replaced with an equally large Horseshoe sign of similar proportions, with decorative horseshoes at the corner piece and along the first floor fascia.

The first "Vegas Vic" sign for the Pioneer Club depicting the image of the smiling cowboy (head only) was erected in 1948. The Vegas Vic image had

originated as part of a promotional campaign created by the Las Vegas Chamber of Commerce in 1945. They hired the J. Walter Thompson advertising agency to boost the city with a national campaign. In 1947, a new firm, the West-Marquis Agency, was hired, and it created the cowboy logo later to known as "Vegas Vic." Soon Vegas Vic became ubiquitous, appearing in billboards and print ads in many western states.

In 1948, inspired by the tourism campaign, the owners of the Pioneer Club hotel and casino, Tutor Scherer, Farmer Page and others obtained the rights to the Vegas Vic image and hired YESCO to fabricate a sign in the likeness of the head of Vegas Vic. Placed on top of the building across the street, the casino-hotel's name was also spelled out in 8-foot-tall letters that were engineered to withstand the potential for 100 mph winds in the Las Vegas

View of Fremont Street circa 1950.
UNLV Library Special Collections.

Valley. In 1951, the Pioneer Club again hired YESCO to design a full-bodied neon Vegas Vic at a cost of $28,000. The 50-foot-tall, 6-ton sign figure designed by Pat Denner and Herman Boernge stood over the Pioneer Club with an animated cigarette, an articulated waving hand, and even a voice box that welcomed tourists with "Howdy Podner!" at 15-minute intervals. Vegas Vic quickly became a successful symbol of the city's casinos and entertainment district. Around the same time, two motels used the Vegas Vic image, the Valley Motel on East Fremont (now gone) and the Nevada Motel (now restored in the Fremont Street Gallery.)

Neon was not only found on casinos and gaming halls during the 1940s, but included nearly every commercial building type. This included the city's new airport. The city's growing population led to the opening of the new McCarran Field airport terminal in 1948. Located on a former airfield located south of the city and the Strip, the airport was named in honor of Nevada Senator Patrick McCarran, a champion of aviation-related development whose efforts became invaluable in securing the airport's establishment. McCarran and others sought to build a modern airport facility to accommodate the town's growing tourism and economic growth fueled by Hoover Dam. The new airport opened with an adobe-style terminal. An entrance gate created by two pylons clad in stone masonry and connected by a large, metal sign arched across the entrance drive greeted travelers driving to the terminal. A metal aircraft propeller outlined in red and white neon was attached to the front of each stone pylon. Atop each pylon was the profile of a bird's wing rendered in metal with an outlined halo of pink neon. McCarran Field's neon-illuminated entrance symbolized modernity and progress for Las Vegas' new age of aviation.

While casinos often boasted the most flamboyant neon signs in Las Vegas' history, many smaller businesses, particularly motels, capitalized on the popular signage early on. The motel and the commercial strip were the architectural models for the early Las Vegas Strip. The typical motel of the 1930s and 1940s stood along the road that led into town. They accommodated the car by allowing plenty of room to drive in and back up to the room. The motor court was U- or L-shaped, opening to the roadway, and registration was nearby. All motor courts had a large sign advertising the motel's amenities, such as air conditioning, a swimming pool, and the nearby attractions.

The Chief Hotel Court opened in 1940 at 1201 East Fremont Street with distinctive pole-mounted signage at the roadside of one of the city's early motor courts. The sign was rendered in multicolored neon featuring an Indian Chief in a white-feathered headdress. The sign is now one of the oldest surviving signs in the city today, and has been restored and installed in The Neon Museum's exhibit on Fremont Street.

Catering to the wedding industry, Dot's Flowers offered both corsages and free wedding information to the would-be bride and groom. This restored sign was created in 1949, and is in place on Fremont.

The Chief Court Hotel on East Fremont Street drew in automobile tourists with its multi-colored neon pole-mounted sign. UNLV Library Special Collections.

McCarran Field entrance gate signage, as seen in ca. 2006. Courtesy of Allen Sandquist.

The Society Cleaners dry cleaning company opened on 8th Street in downtown Las Vegas in 1946. The new business featured a new building-mounted neon sign with artistically composed top hat and cane. Since the establishment's closure in 2006, the sign was donated to The Neon Museum, and is currently on Las Vegas Blvd.

Some of the businesses to emerge in Las Vegas catered to the City's growing and lasting market for fast wedding services. Part of Nevada's tourism trade during the 1940s included the attraction of easy weddings and divorces. Nevada had made itself competitive by reducing its residency requirement from three months to just six weeks in 1931. In 1939,

the Nelson Eddy marriage and the Clark Gable divorce made national headlines and brought new tourists. In 1940, the city even opened a marriage-license bureau in the Union Pacific train depot. Shortly into the decade, World War II began an unprecedented number of marriages and divorces nationwide. During deployment for World War II, military servicemen married in haste before being sent off to sea. Upon returning, many divorced and re-married. The Clark County Recorder's Office illustrates a dramatic rise in weddings and divorces in 1941 and 1942, and again in 1946 and 1947. Motor courts and wedding chapels eager to attract tourists interested in a quickie wedding posted signs advertising wedding information at the roadside.

1950s

In the late 1940s, the state's advertising slogan, "If you can't do it at home, come to Nevada," was an effort to promote gambling and easy marriage and divorce. Las Vegas promoted itself using photographs of bathing beauties posing outside of the new casinos and then ran the ads during the mid-winter months. The campaign promoted the city's hospitality, scenery, and gambling, while boating on Lake Mead and Hoover Dam were billed as bonus side trips. As the new casinos went up in the 1950s, enterprising business owners erected countless motels in other areas of the city to house the tourists.

The 1950s began a time of overwhelming growth in Las Vegas, with the population tripling from 24,624 to 64,405 residents by the close of the decade. New development was encouraged by military expansion, transportation improvements, and tourism marketing campaigns. In 1950, the federal presence in Clark County reemerged when the Atomic Energy Commission opened the

Nevada Test Site for atomic bomb testing 60 miles north of the city, bringing employment opportunities to Las Vegas. Meanwhile, the city began a major advertising campaign to increase tourism, and the casino industry was growing more swiftly than ever. By the mid 1960s, the new Interstate 15 through Las Vegas brought even more residents and tourists from Los Angeles and Salt Lake City leading to improved access and expansion in and around the city.

Las Vegas' boom during the 1950s became a golden age of commercial development in the city. As neon was losing favor in other cities nationwide, it continued

its ascent in Las Vegas. In a competitive period of one-upmanship, casino and hotel signs became more imaginative, more sculptural, and, most of all, larger than ever before. As new casino-hotels opened along Fremont Street and the Strip, each sign carried the potential to become a thematic symbol of the establishment. In turn, many of the distinctive neon signs from the 1950s have since become icons of the town's early period as a regional entertainment capital.

Sign Companies in the 1950s

Through the end of the 1940s, no one single sign manufacturing company dominated the field of

The Flamingo's remodeled ca. 1953 signage, as pictured in a postcard. UNLV Library Special Collections.

Boernge's rendering for the new Desert Inn hotel-casino signage. UNLV Library Special Collections.

advertising in Las Vegas. But in the 1950s, YESCO moved ahead of the competition with their sign designers who author Tom Wolfe called "the designer-sculptor geniuses of Las Vegas". Throughout the 1920s, 1930s, and 1940s, the craftsmen who created the early neon signs came from a variety of sign-manufacturing backgrounds, and were collectively known as commercial sign men.

By the late 1940s, companies such as YESCO also began to hire full-time professional commercial artists. YESCO had the advantage of securing a team comprised of both commercial artists and the Hollywood film industry's set designers and painters. When other sign companies attempted to enter the competitive field of winning contracts for casino signs, YESCO had already established a solid track record for producing creative, attention-grabbing signage in Las Vegas. This is not to say that YESCO did not face increasing competition during the 1950s, however, when other sign companies began to battle for coveted commissions from well-heeled casino owners.

When the production of spectacular signage became big business in Las Vegas in the 1950s, YESCO and the newcomer AD-ART Company established themselves as the two most prolific neon sign manufacturers in Las Vegas. As a result, both companies became the envy of every other neon sign workshop in the nation. When other cities installed ordinances banning the use of neon, Las Vegas permitted artistic freedom beyond that of all other cities. Foremost was experimentation with the incorporation of architecture and neon. As in the project for The Mint in 1957, sign designers often collaborated with the architects hired by the casinos for a unified design scheme.

Las Vegas Club.
UNLV Library Special Collections.

YESCO's signage for the Dunes in 1955. UNLV Library Special Collections.

By the end of the 1950s, the five most active sign companies in Las Vegas were AD-ART Inc., Federal Sign, Heath and Co., Larsen Signs, and YESCO. Most neon sign designers worked at large sign fabrication companies such as these, rather than work independently. These five companies strenuously competed with each other for the same work and clients and fiercely guarded company design concepts. On occasion, companies such as YESCO even had its own artists compete with each other for certain projects.

Presentations to clients were often elaborate in an effort to win over a potential client, frequently including scaled models or films to show animated lights. Once a contract was won, construction and engineering drawings were made, and sometimes working models were used to aid in sign fabrication. Most of the sign's components were made at the sign company's factory to require minimal on-site assembly. The signs were built in modular pieces and then transported to Las Vegas where cranes lifted the signs into place. Installation was conducted either by the sign firm itself, or through a collaborative effort between the sign engineers and the building's architects. Finally, a sign's individual pieces were assembled like a jigsaw puzzle on site. Once a sign was in place, the sign company's responsibilities could include service and maintenance over the life of the sign and even financing.

By the early 1950s, new hotels abandoned the traditional motifs of the American West, such as stone and cattle fences, and took on more exotic styles from the African desert, the Mediterranean coast, or tropical locales. This was in part due to the challenge of appealing to Southern Californians, who constituted the majority of Las Vegas' tourists and for whom the Old Western theme was less exotic or glamorous than the East Coast visitor. Hotel keepers along the

Los Angeles Highway also realized this and adopted alternative themes for their hotels. Nonetheless, many casinos in the Glitter Gulch carried on themes of the Old Frontier nearly to the point of caricature. Among these was the Golden Nugget, which was the gaudiest casino to recreate the old western saloon motif by using imitation 1890-signs, nineteenth century barroom woodwork on the interior, and having its employees dress in western costume. The Fremont Street casinos' sensational atmosphere and their promotion of Old Western theme continued through the 1950s.

YESCO designer Herman Boernge was among a handful of early graphic artists who shaped the signage along the early Strip. When the Desert Inn opened in 1950, the Strip had become a corridor of five resorts that gleamed in metallic signs during the day and glowed in multi-color neon at night. Boernge's sign for the Desert Inn took on a free-form, elliptical shape with the image of a cactus at center, all outlined in

The Mint hotel-casino on Fremont Street.
UNLV Library Special Collections.

YESCO'S Stardust sign in 1958. UNLV Library Special Collections.

neon lighting. Like the Thunderbird before it, the sign sat atop an observation tower formed by the casino's cocktail lounge. A second roadside sign featuring the lettering "Wilbur Clark's Desert Inn" atop the top edge of a roadside entrance archway greeted guests at the highway. The archway's stone-and-wood-beam design was a sophisticated design influenced by the Prairie Style of Frank Lloyd Wright's work. Dominant horizontal lines, flat roofs and edges, and a combination of stone and wood characterize the style as it was conceived for The Desert Inn. The casino-hotel set the new standard for architectural style and design on the Strip for the next decade. The Desert Inn also began a new trend in hotel-casino signage that included designing directional and other secondary signs to match the hotel's logo.

The Sahara casino-hotel opened in 1952 with another sophisticated architectural style that rivaled that of the Desert Inn. The Sahara did not express its theme in its

sign's lettering, which rested on top of the stone and concrete tower that projected from a large base.

To keep up with the competition, in 1953 the Flamingo was remodeled in what the *Las Vegas Sun* called "Aztec Modern." The Flamingo's 1946 signage was replaced with a larger lit sign that was applied to the fascia of a long porch. The "Flamingo" lettering was an unusual and flamboyant rendition of small rings of neon tubing within open-channeled letters. At the same time, The Flamingo erected the tallest freestanding sign on the Strip to date. Dubbed the "Champagne Tower," the cylindrical 60-foot tower was entirely clad in a web of animated neon rings and became the first truly spectacular lighted sign on the Strip. It also prompted the neighboring casinos to update their signs by making signs taller and more visually imposing.

The hotels' increasingly sophisticated sign designs on the Strip in the early 1950s had little bearing on those

of the flamboyant Glitter Gulch. Downtown Las Vegas still carried on the styles and Old Western themes of the 1940s while eschewing the trends adopted by the newer, more stylishly themed hotel-casinos on the Strip. The disparity did not appear to concern the casino owners in either district, however. The Strip largely attracted a new and different clientele than Glitter Gulch. Some casino owners had establishments in both Glitter Gulch and the Strip, and learned to market to the increasingly different clientele that were drawn to the two locations.

During the early 1950s on Fremont Street, neon signage began to evolve from flat, two-dimensional signs and into three dimensions. Casinos also sought taller signs than ever when constructing new buildings by remodeling existing ones. One of the tallest signs first erected on Fremont Street was for the Las Vegas Club. The sign was a vertical blade that soared 120 feet over the corner at Fremont and Main streets. The Las Vegas Club sign remained the tallest in the downtown district for the next decade. When the Lucky Strike Club had the disadvantage of having one of the narrowest building fronts on Fremont Street, it responded to its small street-frontage by creating a narrow but eye-catching sign. For this, YESCO designer Boernge designed a three-dimensional sign in a tall curving wedge featuring a variety of neon patterns and incandescent bulbs to create a brighter sign than its neighbors.

In 1956, YESCO oversaw the remodeling of the Golden Nugget's exterior with signage that turned the façade itself into a new level of sign design. Instead of displaying several separate sign pieces, the new signage covered the entire façade of the old building with what effectively became a new façade in itself. YESCO designer Kermit Wayne created the concept of wrapping the building in a three-story sheathing

The Moulin Rouge signage at the building's tower, as seen in 1955.
UNLV Library Special Collections.

of metal, neon, and incandescent bulbs that swept across the building's façades that faced Fremont and Second streets. At the corner, Wayne designed a 30 x 34-foot curving bullnose that rounded into the entrance marquee in a Western-style baroque display of scrolls and neon stripes. The bullnose "shield" was illuminated in bright letters that read "casino" and horizontal ribbons of yellow neon. Wayne reused the existing 1950 Golden Nugget sign, which was then perched above the new bullnose to a height of 100 feet over the sidewalk. The ends of the building's two façades were bracketed with smaller replicas of the modified 1950 sign. While the Golden Nugget's refacing retained the Old Western style and typeface of the casino's old façade, Wayne's seamless integration of the building and its signage accomplished a larger scale than any other casino had attempted in the Glitter Gulch at the time. The total display resulted in the first coordinated, unified blend of architecture, theme, and advertisement that became ubiquitous from that point forward in Las Vegas. In the 1960s, the Golden Nugget bought out its neighbors and again hired YESCO to design an extension of the same design motif across the entire block, including a second bullnose and matching surmounted sign at the corner of First and Fremont streets.

Wayne's concept for the Golden Nugget quickly became the envy of the Glitter Gulch, and sign designers copied his design for the bullnose signage. Although the three-dimensional curved corner had been used for theater marquees in Las Vegas before then, Wayne's design was the first to bring the shape to Fremont Street. The Golden Nugget's traveling yellow bulbs were also an example of a renewed interest in incandescent lamps by the mid-1950s. After years of creating signs that only employed neon, sign designers were starting to combine both colored

The illuminated Anderson Dairy sign. Nevada State Museum.

incandescent bulbs and neon in their signage, often using a vigorous display of chasing or flashing bulbs to complement neon tubing.

Beyond Glitter Gulch, neon signs advertised countless shops and small businesses in Las Vegas in the 1950s. Local businesses like Anderson Dairy announced the company's name with large, metal signage and bold neon attached to its building facade. The mascot "Andy" Anderson, the milkman, was featured atop

Golden Nugget 1970s. Nevada State Museum.

Sahara Hotel smaller sign. UNLV Library Special Collections.

a bull's eye logo. YESCO produced Anderson Dairy's distinctive sign, which adorned the plant's rooftop from 1956 until 1994. The "Andy" Anderson sign component is currently installed on Fremont Street; the rest of the sign components are housed at The Neon Museum.

Neon lighting took on a particular resonance in Las Vegas and in other parts of the open landscape of the Southwest. Without many trees or buildings, the illuminated neon sign could be seen from miles away in the evening. Western motels used the neon medium perhaps more than any other business. This was also perhaps afforded by the low profile of casino and motel buildings when casinos within Las Vegas' city limits were once limited to two stories. The low, horizontal profile has allowed building-mounted signs to be seen at longer distances. Traveling north on the Strip, the neon glow of Las Vegas acted as a beacon signaling toward the city.

In contrast with the façade-mounted signs in the compact density of the pedestrian-oriented downtown of the Fremont Street casino district, resorts along the Strip were widely spaced and catered more to the automobile tourists driving along Las Vegas Boulevard South (also known as Highway 91, or The Strip). It was no accident that the first casinos were located along the highway that originally connected Las Vegas to Los Angeles, from which many of the visitors originated. Instead of building-fronted signs, businesses utilized tall, freestanding pylons that could be seen from long distances—as far as a mile away. The buildings along the Strip were set far apart from

Free-standing pylon by AD-ART, 1968. Building façade signwork by YESCO, 1958. Clark County Museum.

one another and were surrounded by parking lots. The lots in between the large casinos on South Las Vegas Boulevard gradually became populated with smaller businesses such as wedding chapels, gas stations, smaller motels, and other establishments that catered to the tourism trade. As more hotels and other roadside businesses began to fill in the gaps, signage too began to increase and compete for attention. Before long, five of the six tallest signs in the world were standing along the shoulders of Las Vegas Boulevard. Although signage on the Strip was large, it typically lacked the ornate flamboyance of the Glitter Gulch in favor of popular architectural tastes and the influence of simplified Modern aesthetics.

In 1955, the Dunes casino and resort opened on the Strip with theatrical signage featuring the largest thematic figure on the Strip to date. Above a modified wedge-shaped sign that read "Dunes" on both sides, a 30-foot-tall, fully dimensional sculpture of a Sultan constructed of steel and fiberglass loomed above the entrance porte-cochere.

Designed by YESCO's Ben Mitchem, the Sultan extended the precedent of the Thunderbird's perched birds. Flood lights illuminated the impressive figure at night, contributing to the theatrically illuminated entertainment palaces emerging along the sides of the Strip.

The Tropicana opened at the south end of the Strip in 1957 with a building designed by architect M. Tony Sherman of Miami. In the fashion of its contemporaries, the Tropicana featured a prominent roadside sign that announced the casino's tropical theme. The grounds featured a neon-outlined, tulip-shaped fountain and an outdoor pool with underwater music. The building itself continued the motel-style archetype, with flanking two-story wings that housed banks of guest rooms.

The Mint hotel and casino opened in 1957 across from the Golden Nugget on Fremont Street, and raised the bar for a spectacular combination of three-dimensional signage and architecture. Owner Del Webb hired YESCO designers to work in partnership with the building's

architects, Zick and Sharp, to produce an unusual, eye-catching design. Their collaborative concept called for a large, arched canopy that began at ground level at one side of the building and swept across its façade in a broad arch, turning skyward into a vertical blade sign at the opposite side, with the lettering "The Mint" in vertical, stacked form. A 16-foot-wide, 6-point star outlined in neon surmounted the top of the blade as a beacon. Two steel I-beams supported the entire canopy and blade sign, the load of which was diverted to the building's reinforced concrete structure.

Altogether, the Mint's sculptural sign with its streamlined design was more Modern in style than any other establishment on Fremont Street. It was the first building in the district to embrace many Modern principles, such as asymmetrical sign and emphasis on geometrical structural form. The building's large flat-roofed curves with straight edges, and its use of concrete materials was integral to the architecture of the building. Moreover, its graphic lighting design lacked references to historical styles such as ornate decoration and references to Old Western themes. Even the neon employed emphasized Modern design, as the blade and canopy were entirely clad in repetitive fuchsia-colored horizontal neon stripping, edged with a band of small, white incandescent bulbs in tight courses. This ribbon of hot pink and white light was activated to illuminate in a sweeping chase sequence from end to end. Underneath the arching canopy at the façade, a second canopy above the first story was shaped in a horizontal wave as it supported the second "The Mint" lettering. A grid of lighted polka dots decorated the building's recessed façade wall behind both canopies. The Mint's sculptural façade was arguably the most avant-garde design on Fremont Street at the time.

In 1958, YESCO's design for the new Stardust casino-hotel signage set a record for the most massive sign

on the Strip. YESCO designer Kermit Wayne designed the famous Stardust sign that set a new precedent for theatricality and monumental size. A collage of neon, incandescent lights, three-dimensional planets, comets, and cosmic rays, the sign stretched 216 feet and rose 27 feet above the first story of the casino. Space Age theme was popular in 1958, the year after Russian satellite Sputnik orbited around the earth, kicking the United States' race to space into full gear and sparking a wave of popular imagery to follow. In response, the Stardust's cosmic-inspired lettering sparkled in 11,000 flashing bulbs and 7,000 feet of neon tubing. The angular style of the "STARDUST" lettering came to be called the "Atomic" font. Plastic spheres in the shapes of satellites and

planets were shaped from acrylic plastic and framed a large, glowing "earth" sphere that was 16-feet in diameter. Observers reported being able to see the Stardust's sign from almost three miles away across the desert landscape. A second, slightly smaller sign with the same Atomic Stardust lettering stood at the roadway along with an illuminated readerboard advertising the casino's Lido de Paris dancing show. Other hotels on the Strip explored the realm of large, glitteringly illuminated signs, such as the Flamingo's Champagne Tower, but, as the Golden Nugget's 1956 façade remodeling did on Fremont Street, the Stardust sign was the first on the Strip to also become incorporated into the architecture of the building façade itself.

The Stardust sign was actually a design solution to the problem of covering up an uninteresting building façade, which was the concept of the "decorated shed" discussed in the 1972 publication *Learning from Las Vegas* by Robert Venturi, Denise Scott Brown and Steven Izenour. Behind its large sign, there was little that made the Stardust architecturally appealing. The complex of buildings was an assembly of motels that stretched out in wings encompassing 1,000 rooms. Before the sign was conceived, Stardust's architecture had no unifying theme or architectural style. The project was also delayed two years when the owner Tony Cornero died unexpectedly from a heart attack in 1955. It was picked up by Moe Dalitz, Allard Roen and others from the Desert Inn, who quickly discovered

Del Mar Motel postcard. Nevada State Museum, Las Vegas.

that the chaos of the construction needed rescuing. The new owners' direction salvaged the buildings and managed to complete the resort with the help of a large team of architects and designers. In the end, the disarray of the plain buildings that came to be the Stardust was saved by YESCO's design for a large

sign that covered the second and third floors of the front building. Their concept was to attach what was essentially a sparkling billboard to a relatively plain structure to cover it up and at the same time, instill theatricality and the cosmic theme to the building through its Atomic lettering and Space-Age imagery.

Following the Stardust, many signs along the Strip began to replace their signs with larger ones, some of which were even bigger than the two or three-story buildings behind them.

At a time when all of the hotels on the Las Vegas Strip

were racially segregated, the Moulin Rouge Casino opened in West Las Vegas in May 1955. In the *Las Vegas Review Journal*, advertisements billed the Rouge as "the nation's first major inter-racial hotel."

Unlike the other casinos, black entertainers and guests could stay at Moulin Rouge. Heavyweight champion Joe Louis greeted visitors, and from the start, the club had sold-out shows that attracted A-list entertainers such as Pearl Bailey, Harry Belafonte, Tallulah Bankhead, Nat King Cole, and Sammy Davis, Jr. The Moulin Rouge's sign featured stylized, cursive script and was designed by Western Neon's Betty Willis. Despite the casino's success, the Moulin Rouge shut down after only five months of operation under uncertain circumstances. After remaining shuttered for nearly fifty years, the building burned in 2003. The Moulin Rouge's characteristically stylish neon signage, however, survived the blaze and is in the Neon Museum's Boneyard.

Moulin Rouge sign designer Willis is best known for her iconic 1959 design for the "Welcome to Fabulous Las Vegas, Nevada" sign in the median of South Las Vegas Boulevard. The sign has become the symbol of Las Vegas ever since its installation at the south end of the Strip, and is now listed on the National Register of Historic Places.

Motels
As the new casinos went up in the 1950s, countless motels were erected in other areas of the city to house the tourists. The Del Mar Motel opened in 1953 at 1411 S. Las Vegas Boulevard in Las Vegas with a sign designed by Willis. The Del Mar Motel's distinctive neon feature was that it could be seen from both directions, which was a popular design approach at the time. The Del Mar Motel sign remained in place until the establishment was demolished in 2005, and

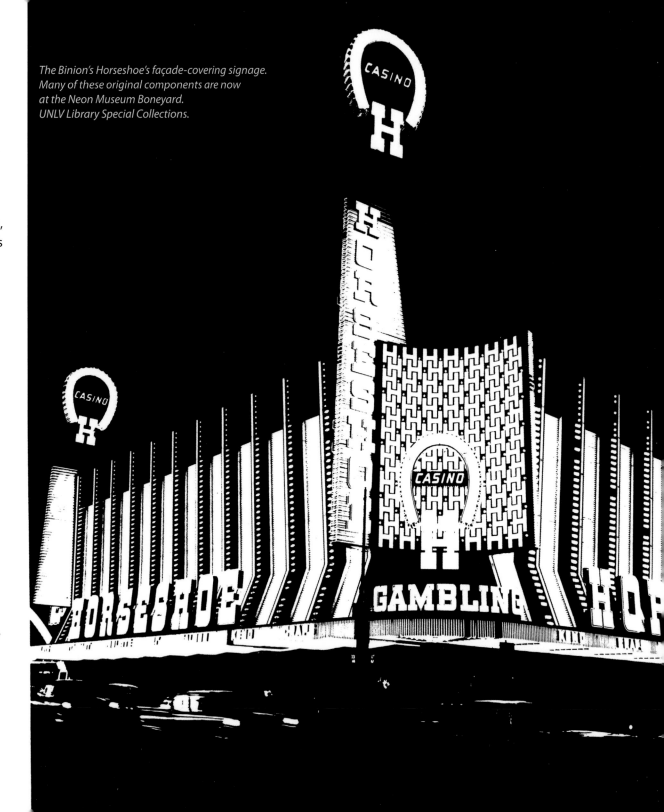

The Binion's Horseshoe's façade-covering signage. Many of these original components are now at the Neon Museum Boneyard.
UNLV Library Special Collections.

The 1948 Thunderbird with its original signage. Courtesy of Dorothy Wright.

the sign components were relocated to The Neon Museum Boneyard.

Outside the hotel industry, as Las Vegas experienced an intense period of growth and expansion during the 1950s, residents began new businesses to meet the demands of the growing community. The Anderson Dairy, the oldest established dairy at that time, followed suit by enlarging its dairy plant. In 1956, after operating for nearly 50 years since 1907, Anderson Dairy built a new processing plant in what was believed to be the largest and most state-of-the-art dairy in the Southwest region of the United States. The company moved its operations from 1440 Las Vegas Boulevard South to 801 Searles Avenue, due north of Las Vegas'

old downtown. Plans for the new buildings included a large, neon sign on top announcing "Anderson Dairy" in red and white neon.

Anderson Dairy commissioned YESCO to design the business' new sign. YESCO's scheme for Anderson Dairy was a characteristically polished composition of balanced lettering and an eye-catching image, such as the red-and-white bull's-eye cabinet. Herman Boernge adapted the cartoon "Andy" Anderson milkman, the company's mascot, into the signage and rendered it in red neon to complement the yellow lettering below it. The sign was installed atop the tallest building at the new Anderson plant in a building-mounted display that extended up from the roof of the building. The

Anderson Dairy sign remained in place until 1994, when the plant was remodeled and expanded, and the signage was relocated to The Neon Museum Boneyard. It was then restored and installed on Fremont Street. Anderson Dairy continues to operate at the Searles Avenue location and is the oldest locally owned and operated dairy processing plant in the Las Vegas Valley.

The El Portal Theatre added a new neon blade sign to its marquee in 1953. The Theatre opened in 1928 on Fremont Street as the first theater in Las Vegas. In 1953, the building was renovated with concrete and brick walls, and likely added its new signage at the front of the building at that time with an upright sign outlining "El Portal" in red neon. The El Portal Theatre's blade sign was removed around 1994 when Fremont Street was covered by the "Fremont Street Experience" canopy.

1960s

Nationwide prosperity in the 1960s led to the construction of new casinos and resort hotels in the Las Vegas Valley. By then Las Vegas had established a strong, visual urban framework. The motels of the 1950s developed into larger complexes with theaters, convention centers, and high-rise expansions. The casino signage grew larger and with more sophisticated designs, and this ultimately changed the urban landscape of the Strip and Glitter Gulch. Flashy and increasingly more imaginative signs helped casinos get the attention of tourists along the Strip, but they also served a pragmatic purpose of guiding traffic and announcing shows and activities to guests.

As the 1950s passed into the 1960s, plastic materials and plastic-fronted readerboards illuminated by fluorescent lights began to eclipse the use of neon tubing in the sign industry. Cast acrylic sheet plastic could be used in a variety

Aladdin 1970s. UNLV Library Special Collections.

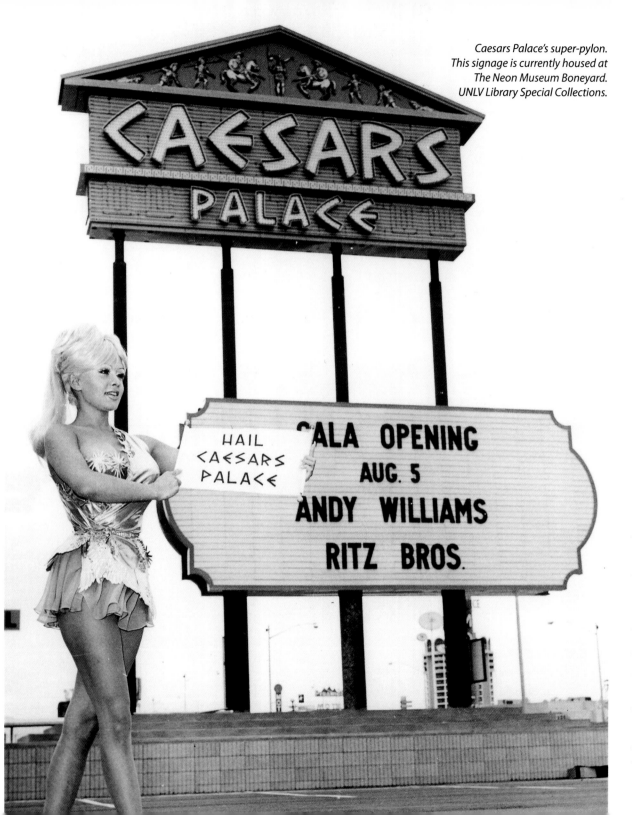

of ways that threatened the popularity of neon in Las Vegas. YESCO was among the sign companies to invest in early plastic manufacturing. However, while plastic light boxes did outpace neon lighting across the nation, the distinctive colored tubes of neon continued to be used extensively in neon signage throughout the 1950s and 1960s.

The casino-hotels on the Strip favored roadside signs that could be easily viewed from a moving vehicle. Consequently, these signs became larger and taller, competing for the fleeting attention of automobile passengers. Robert Venturi, Denise Scott Brown, and Steven Izenour observed this behavior and its affect on Las Vegas' signage and buildings in their influential 1972 publication *Learning From Las Vegas*. The authors reported a two-part type of signage along the Strip. The first type was the large, tall sign that announced the casino or hotel name and could be read quickly from long distances on the highway. The second type was a smaller and lower sign that was read at closer distances and usually contained changeable copy that included the name of the current show or evening special. These signs were commonly called "readerboards" and were among the first signs to utilize the plastic-faced light boxes internally illuminated by fluorescent lighting. The plastic fronts featured rails to hold the changeable clip-on lettering. During the first decades of their use, the readerboard rarely exceeded 10 feet in height and 18-inch lettering.

The 1960s represented a time of unprecedented creativity in sign design. The competition between sign manufacturing firms and between casinos in Las Vegas only increased, and each wanted to be credited with the most eye-catching design. Signs became more elaborate in design complexity and soared to new heights to become the tallest freestanding signs in the world.

The Landmark Hotel and Casino, bought by Howard Hughes and finally opened July 1, 1969. UNLV Library Special Collections.

In the early 1960s, the influence of the enormous, façade-cloaking Stardust signage found its way to Fremont Street where large casino signs began to all but consume buildings. Many casinos in Glitter Gulch remodeled their façades to suit the late Modern fashion of the 1960s. As the former Art Deco or Victorian ornamentation was removed, metal screens with washes of neon lights went up. At the same time, the tall, high-rise form emerged as a new building type in Las Vegas in the early 1960s in Glitter Gulch and on the Strip. This usually took place in the form of the high-rise addition to an existing building, and the towers became taller with time. In 1963, the Fremont Hotel added an addition rising 14 stories, only to be followed by the Mint's new 26-story tower. Along with the soaring stories, neon signs continued to grow larger each year, credited to numerous sign artists of the period.

YESCO designers Ben Mitchem and Jack Larsen, Sr., became two of the most sought-after sign designers among Las Vegas' casino market in the 1960s from their contributions to the new Binion's Horseshoe signage on Fremont Street. For the remodeling of Binion's Horseshoe, the architects, Wayne McAllister and William Wagner, handpicked design elements from Mitchem and Larsen's design submissions to create a collaborative effort between all four designers. The result was a unified design spectacular that echoed that of the 1956 Golden Nugget façade remodel, but on a taller, larger scale. The composition called for a concave "bullnose" at one corner of the block-long building, which held a 13-foot horseshoe and a 7-foot letter "H," in front of a 31-foot-tall panel of interlocking neon "H" letters behind it. This was contrasted by a convex canopy underneath the panel, which held the word "gambling." At one side of the bullnose, a tall blade side rose with the vertical letters "horseshoe," a second horseshoe motif, and an "H" at the apex. This entire assemblage was repeated at the opposite corner of the building.

The Neon Museum exhibited the restored 1966 Aladdin's lamp on Fremont Street.

The canopy and the blade sign were both covered in horizontal rows of white neon tubing, creating a bright glow. In fact, the entire canopy that ran along the long side of the building on Fremont Street was swathed in horizontal white neon tubing, lighting the sidewalk below it. In between the corners, the Horseshoe's Fremont Street-facing wall was windowless and covered in more horizontal turquoise neon tubing that was interrupted by thin, evenly spaced vertical pilasters that served to visually break up the mass of neon light. By

one estimate, over 40,000 feet of neon tubing were used on the Binion's Horseshoe façade and it was touted as the largest neon sign in the world.

In 1964, the California-based firm AD-ART arrived to Las Vegas and posed the first serious competition to YESCO. The following year, they officially entered the competition of neon sign design on the Strip with their new signs for the Thunderbird, the Flamingo, and Stardust. For the Thunderbird, AD-ART updated the existing signage by adapting the casino's bird image into a stylized eagle outlined in animated neon that created the illusion of the bird flying atop a tall, wedge-shaped pylon sign that was lit in horizontal neon tubing. The pylon included v-shaped signage with two readerboards per side to display the casino's current attractions. To the Thunderbird's building, AD-ART designed a long, 560-foot-wide, 24-foot-tall sign that covered the entire facade in panels of metal, waffle-patterned sheets and held 12-foot-tall "Thunderbird" lettering rendered in open-channel neon. The color scheme featured alternating teal-blue and green backgrounds. A new porte-cochere that was added to the front of the building with one of the former Thunderbird figures on top of it. The all-encompassing signage was a continuation of the large-scale, façade sheathing pioneered by the 1958 Stardust.

By 1963, even the five-year-old Stardust was undergoing remodeling, as the casino added a nine-story tower at its north side. More innovative was the new, 31-story Landmark Hotel tower built in 1964. Howard Hughes later bought the unfinished project in 1969. The bar, restaurant, and casino were placed at the observation deck at the top, mimicking the futuristic Space Needle from Seattle's 1962 World's Fair. It was never successful and closed in 1990. Later the Landmark implosion was included in the 1995 movie "Mars Attacks."

In 1964, the 1955 Dunes casino-hotel gained a diamond-shaped tower called Diamond of the Dunes by architect Milton Schwartz of Chicago. The Diamond of the Dunes was 21 stories of concrete slabs, with rooms setback from the balconies to provide both shade and outdoor spaces. Unlike its neighboring casinos, the Dunes had a long-range plan that would transform the complex into a mega-resort with plans for five additional towers.

In the downtown, the Four Queens casino also opened its

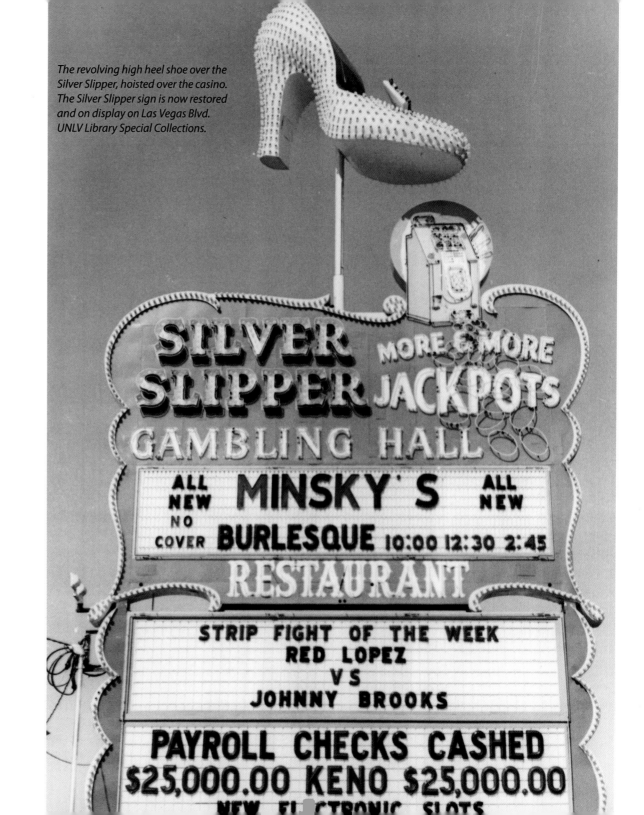

The revolving high heel shoe over the Silver Slipper, hoisted over the casino. The Silver Slipper sign is now restored and on display on Las Vegas Blvd. UNLV Library Special Collections.

The Stardust's ca. 1968 super-pylon signage. Since the casino's closing in 2006, all of the Stardust's sign components are now located in The Neon Museum Boneyard. UNLV Library Special Collections.

doors at the corner of Casino Center and Fremont Streets, becoming the fourth casino of the so-called "Famous Foursome" of the Glitter Gulch: Four Queens, Golden Nugget, Binion's Horseshoe, and the Fremont Hotel.

Many planned visions of casino architecture went unrealized in Las Vegas in the 1960s, usually from the lack of financing to back them. After nine years without any new casinos in Las Vegas in 1966 two new operations opened on the Strip: the Aladdin and Caesars Palace. The new Caesars Palace (intentionally spelled without the apostrophe) was designed in an opulent Ancient Roman theme created by long rows of copies of Classical statuary, fountains, and cypress trees along the entrance drive leading to the building's porte-cochere. Unlike other casinos along the Strip, parking was relegated to the sides to create the formal approach. The Caesars Palace building itself was a 14-story convex tower with symmetrical wings that curved toward the street frontage, resonant of the elliptical colonnade of St. Peter's Square in Rome.

The fact that the Caesars Palace colonnade and its many other architectural references pointed more to Baroque Rome than to Ancient Rome some 1600 years prior did not matter to its architects or to the patrons. The primary goal among themed casinos was to tantalize the imagination rather than reproduce accurate historical replicas. Many of the architectural devices used were also borrowed from contemporary master architects of Formalism (also referred to as the Ballet Style) of the 1960s. The stylistic approach of Formalism softened the edges of Modern architecture by combining abstract and geometric forms derived from Classical architecture, such as simple semicircular arches or thin colonnades rendered in uncarved white stone. Although the Caesars Palace complex stood out on the Strip with its 135-foot setback that allowed for the dramatic

entrance, the casino-hotel followed the motel model of its neighbors. Behind the entrance façade, motel rooms were aligned along low-story, outstretched wings that faced a pool. Like the other casinos, Caesars Palace also used a prominent pylon sign at the Strip's roadside.

Competition was fierce for the commission of the Caesars Palace signage. Design firms YESCO, AD-ART, and Federal Sign battled over their competing design presentations. Although all three companies featured similar Greco-Roman themes, AD-ART won the contract and created a final sign design that combined elements from all three firms' proposals. YESCO's design was the first choice but they couldn't agree on the financial terms. One element of YESCO's design model was several six inch dimestore toys depicting Roman centurions to show the scale. Caesars liked them so much, they asked that the figures be built in fiberglass.

The finished Caesars Palace sign became one of the more elegant pylon signs on the Strip. It was a combination of ancient Greek and Roman styles, composed of a larger triangular pediment with engaged statuary in the tympanum. The pediment crowned a classical entablature with large, Greek-styled lettering spelling "Caesars" on the frieze and "Palace" on the architrave below it. Both the frieze and architrave were striated with horizontal neon tubing. The entire sign was supported by four tall, fluted columns with ionic capitals. Three of the column shafts were interrupted by a large, sign-marquee. The columns surmounted square plinths on a stepped stereobate platform, on which five life-sized fiberglass Roman soldiers that stood at the base to enhance Roman theme. Although Caesars Palace's theme intended to recall the height of Ancient Roman Empire, many of the architectural design elements used for Caesars Palace were also Ancient

Vegas Vic sign, by YESCO, installed 1951. Nevada State Museum.

Kerkorian's International Hotel entrance.
Courtesy of Allen Sandquist.

Greek architectural motifs. The blending of the styles represented how romanticized images and allusions that evoked the popular imagination was the goal of the architectural and sign designers alike.

The new Aladdin hotel was also hotly contested between the YESCO and AD-ART sign design firms. YESCO won the competition with a three-sided pylon featuring a sculpture of a revolving genie's lamp as its crowning pinnacle. The lamp was covered in yellow incandescent bulbs on all sides, creating a glowing icon for the "Arabian nights" themed casino. The Aladdin also was among the first casinos to fully

integrate its lettered signage into its porte-cochere. The edge of the entrance canopy featured a geometric scallop that followed the edge of the letters "Aladdin," which were large and outlined in neon. The edge of the porte-cochere was outlined in a tight grid of incandescent bulbs. This emphasis on the porte-cochere would be a precursor to the full realization of the porte-cochere-as-signage achieved by the MGM Grand seven years later. YESCO also won the sign concept for the Circus Circus casino in 1967. The design was for a sign that formed a circular fascia encircling the top of the hotel's big top merry-go-round.

Meanwhile, AD-ART won the opportunity to redesign signs for the Frontier (formerly the Last Frontier, followed by the New Frontier). The new sign was a 184-foot-tall pylon that encased a giant, rotating, stylized letter "F" at the top of it. About midway up the pylon, was a horizontal marquee with the name "Frontier." Readerboards were located at the lowest section of the pylon nearest to automobile traffic.

The Silver Slipper casino opened in 1950 on the grounds of the Last Frontier Village along the early Las Vegas Strip. YESCO created the establishment's eye-catching icon in the early 1950s. The slipper was moved to the street to

The La Concha Motel lobby in place on the Strip. The motel building was demolished in 2003, and the lobby was dismantled and relocated at the Neon Museum. The motel neon signage is now located in the museum's boneyard.
Las Vegas News Bureau Photo and Film Archives.

feet to be the tallest sign in the world for the decade following.

The installation of large roadside signage required careful orchestration by the sign fabrication company. Tall pylons required substantial excavation at the site to support the massive weight of a large sign. The largest foundations for signs like the 188-foot-tall Stardust pylon called for foundations as large as 16 to 20 feet in girth. A superstructure of steel I-beams, steel re-bar, and concrete held the sign in place. After the base was set, cranes began to assemble the large pieces of the sign from the manufacturing plant. Firms such as YESCO and Federal Sign (later SSI) maintained offices and shops in Las Vegas, but AD-ART and Heath and Co. shipped their sign components from their main base of operations in California. The individual pieces of the sign would be assembled at the site and then carefully lifted into place by the crane. All of the sign's lamps, neon, and internal wiring were set in place prior to installation.

While the Stardust sign was in fabrication, AD-ART was busy completing the new and improved signs for the Flamingo and the Bonanza Hotel and Casino on the strip. AD-ART's sign for the Bonanza simply read the name "Bonanza" in Victorian Western font surrounded by bulbs and neon outlines. Western Victorian-era scrolls decorated the readerboard below it. In an effort to draw tourists, at the ground level of the pylon, life-size fiberglass figures of cowboys in western clothing simulated a gun-fight scene from the OK corral. The Western theme was making a comeback to the Las Vegas Strip.

In 1967, airline magnate Kirk Kerkorian bought the Flamingo for $13 million, and with this action entered the exclusive milieu of Las Vegas casino owners and influential leaders of the powerful Strip. Kerkorian's first change to the Flamingo was the demolition of its 1953

top the marquee in the 1960s. After many years in the Boneyard, the Slipper was restored and placed across the street from the Neon Museum.

In 1968, after a period of intense competition for the project, AD-ART also won the opportunity to create the Stardust casino and hotel's second generation of iconic signage. The Stardust was located due north of the Frontier, and it was not to be outdone by the Frontier's new, tall pylon sign. In response, AD-ART created a new sign to replace existing roadside sign with a much taller, 188-foottall pylon sign that featured the letters "Stardust" surrounded by a fuschia cloud with a glittering halo of multicolored, four-point stars that twinkled from top to bottom in lighted animation. The

Stardust's celestial theme and Atomic typeface was a continuation of YESCO's original 1958 design. The entire cloud was supported by two tall piers that also held a large readerboard below the clouds and stars. The sign was the most popular sign among Las Vegas residents and tourists alike for many years.

AD-ART's 1968 Stardust commission represented a major coup in the competition for high-profile work in Las Vegas. Staff designer, Paul Miller, won the prestigious General Electric Trophy for the Stardust design's exceptional achievement in electric signage. At that time, Las Vegas had the three tallest neon signs in the world, as the Dunes' sign rose to 180 feet, the Frontier's sign rose to 184 feet, and the Stardust's sign rose to 188

Champagne Tower. He then added a new and larger porte-cochere and a theater, and extended the casino hall closer to the sidewalk to utilize the property's increasingly limited space. AD-ART's new sign for the Flamingo was a roadside pylon, which had become the norm for every major casino by that time. The sign rested on a tall column lighted in vertical strands of pink, red, and white, and unfolded into scalloped waves of the neon in illusion of feathers behind the name "Flamingo." In the end, the Flamingo was simply a training ground for Kerkorian's grander vision of building his new casino-hotel, the International.

One block east of the Strip along Paradise Road, Kerkorian planned the International, a 30-story-tall, 1,500-room tower that was christened the largest hotel in the world. The building featured three wings shaped by three concave exterior walls. AD-ART designers collaborated with the building's architect Martin Stern, Jr., to create tall columns of bulbs and ribbed neon that emphasized the building's dramatic height. A neon grid wrapped the penthouse of the building and continuously unveiled the name "International" in neon. Near the lower part of the building, large, three-part readerboards sprawled horizontally across each of the three facades. Over 180 interior signs adorned the inside of the International, making it the largest sign project in Las Vegas to date at that time. The hotel, later the Hilton, was the home of Elvis, who performed there in the 1970s.

Motels of the Fifties and Sixties

Aiming to house the steady stream of tourists, new motels and renovation projects kept architects, sign designers, and construction businesses busy through the 1960s. In 1961, the La Concha Motel, designed by Paul Revere Williams, opened on the Strip in the memorable form of a dramatically arched lobby

entrance in the shape of a clam shell, which was attached to the front of a long motel row behind it. (The La Concha lobby was moved to the Neon Museum site in 2006.) The La Concha sign repeated the trademark three-arched shell, with a towering "motel" rising above it.

Although the Desert Rose Motel opened at 4000 South Las Vegas Boulevard in 1953, the motel added its billboard-style roadside sign in 1960. The Desert Rose Motel operated on the strip until 1995, when the building was demolished. Its sign was donated to the Neon Museum .

Many other motels opened in the 1950s, or received new signs in the 1950s. Betty Willis, designer of the Welcome sign, recalled creating signs for several motels on and off Las Vegas Boulevard, including the Normandie Motel, the Bow & Arrow, and City Center, among others. The Normandie and Bow & Arrow are part of the outdoor display on Las Vegas Blvd. north of Stewart, and the City Center is in the Neon Boneyard. A local favorite on East Fremont Street designed by Willis was the Blue Angel Motel, with the Blue Onion Drive-In next door. The Blue Onion was a popular hang-out for teens who were finished with their night of cruising Fremont Street.

Wedding Chapels

As Las Vegas gained national appeal as a resort locale for gaming, the wedding service industry benefited from the city's burgeoning notoriety as an entertainment

Welcome sign 1960s. UNLV Library Special Collections.

capital with easy marriage laws. By the early 1960s, the year the Night and Day Wedding Chapel opened, the wedding industry was firmly established in the city. According to a 1968 historic photograph, the Candlelight Wedding Chapel sign originated atop the building housing the Night and Day Wedding Chapel, which was located on the north end of the Las Vegas Strip near the Riviera casino-hotel. The Night and Day chapel is believed to have opened in the early 1960s, and is one of the many wedding ceremony businesses to cater to the demand for quickie weddings in Las Vegas. Sometime

The Night and Day Chapel signage, renovated and installed as the Candlelight Wedding Chapel sign. The signage is currently housed in The Neon Museum Boneyard. Las Vegas News Bureau Photo and Film Archives.

The former Night and Day Chapel, as seen in 1968. Las Vegas News Bureau Photo and Film Archives.

thereafter, the Night and Day Wedding Chapel signage was relocated to the All Religions Wedding Chapel building, which was later renamed the Candlelight Wedding Chapel. The sign's light box was modified and replaced with a re-lettered plastic front during each relocation to reflect changes in name, but otherwise, the sign remained intact. The sign stayed in place until the Candlelight Wedding Chapel sold the property and loaned the sign to The Neon Museum. The Candlelight Wedding Chapel building was moved to the Clark County Museum, 1830 S. Boulder Highway in Henderson, where it was restored and is part of their collection of historic buildings that are open to the public.

1970s

Shortly after the realization of the lighted superpylon sign along the Strip, the porte-cochere became the next and perhaps the most architectural form of lighted signage in Las Vegas among the heavyweight casino-hotel ventures. Although the porte-cochere serves the functional purpose of an entrance shelter for vehicles dropping off guests at the building's front entrance, this newfound emphasis on the architectural feature was inspired more by the structure's potential as a dazzling spectacle of incandescent lamps and neon to beckon both pedestrians and automobile travelers toward a casino-hotel's entrance. In conceptualizing the illuminated porte-cochere, many architects collaborated with sign designers to conceive the casino-hotel as a coordinated work of art, whose goal was to increase visitor traffic.

In 1973, Kerkorian's new MGM Grand Hotel introduced Las Vegas' first grandiose porte-cochere on the south end of the Strip. The building itself was the largest hotel in the world, accommodating 2,100 rooms in polished gold and green finishes in the theme of the old Hollywood film industry glamour. MGM's architect, Martin Stern, Jr., designed the porte-cochere to be the focal point of the

The Desert Rose Motel sign on the strip. The sign is now housed at The Neon Museum Boneyard. Las Vegas News Bureau Photo and Film Archives. Nevada State Museum.

building's sleek, glass-faced Modern architecture. AD-ART produced the signage with a modernized version of MGM's famous lion logo. The "MGM Grand" lettering on the building's façade, however, was a subdued departure from the dazzling lights from the 1960s. The letters were dark, back-lit from lights set behind the letters to give them a haunting silhouetted look. Moreover, the letters were mounted to the building's exterior wall, which meant that they only rose to half the height of the tallest pylon signs on the Strip at the time. In effect, the typical pylon sign that announced the casino-hotel's name was de-emphasized in favor of the extravagant, nonverbal signage of the port-cochere.

While the first porte-cocheres along the Strip were small in size, perhaps large enough to cover one or two

automobiles, MGM's canopy was expansive and became the focal point of the entire building. A gridded ceiling of gold bulbs and reflective bronze finishes illuminated the space, and the area underneath it became an extension of the interior of the casino. Opposite to the entrance into the building was a pool with dramatically lit statuary and broad staircases leading to the porte-cochere. The look was glitzy but elegant, in the high-fashion mode of Beverly Hills' opulence. The light emanating from the new porte-cochere became the new beacon to draw both pedestrian visitors and those arriving by car to the front entrance of the casino. MGM Grand's entrance effectively became the model for the shift from the tall pylon to the porte-cochere along South Las Vegas Boulevard. In 1975, a year after the MGM Grand opened, the Moorish-themed Aladdin began on a renovation that included a performing arts center and a $250,000 porte-cochere designed by AD-ART's Charles Barnard.

The MGM Grand raised the standard of sophisticated sign design on the Strip in Las Vegas. However, it also marked an end of an era of growth and expansion among casino-hotels during the 1960s until the mid-1970s. It took another 15 years before new casinos would arrive to the Strip and to Fremont Street. Meanwhile, high-rise additions in Las Vegas began to resemble Modern corporate architecture. This aesthetic often produced bland results including buildings of concrete and steel, unadorned fascias, and otherwise plain façades. These plain steel-and-concrete designs were in stark contrast with the glittering extravaganzas of neon and incandescent bulb raceways of the Golden Nugget and Binion's Horseshoe that persisted on Fremont Street.

While neon lighting was used frequently during the heated sign competition of the 1960s, neon signage and fabrication had fallen from favor nationwide during this time, with the exception of Times Square in New York, which was a tourist-attraction anomaly in the same way that Las Vegas had been. However, neon lighting gained a small resurgence in the commercial market nationwide during the late 1970s when discotheques began to open and revive a new demand for neon. Neon lighting seemed to match the flamboyant colors of the flashy disco fad. When casino and hotel development slowed in the in late 1970s, Las Vegas' new discos brought a small market to the neon sign fabrication industry. Perhaps in response to this, in 1975, YESCO opened a new production facility on South Cameron Street, Las Vegas, and the company's sales hit an all time high.

Few of the casinos carried on the creative tradition of the neon spectaculars from the 1960s. The Flamingo added a multi-colored three-dimensional sign rendered in large Flamingo feathers in 1976. That same year, the Circus Circus added "Lucky" the clown, which was a large,

In 1980, The Sahara's new 220-foot sign became the world's tallest free-standing pylon in the world at the time. The Sahara pylon is now located in The Neon Museum Boneyard. UNLV Library Special Collections.

two-sided clown that pointed down toward the circus tent, nearly in the mode of the original waving Vegas Vic. The sign also was notable for fully incorporating the readerboard into the sign's imagery, as the body of the clown rather than a semi-attached component. YESCO won the commission for the sign. The Sahara's new sign, installed in 1978, became the largest free-standing, super-pylon sign in the world, rising 220 feet.

1980s

A new era of casino development and management emerged in the 1980s when large hotel corporations began to buy the older casinos on the Strip. Architecturally, hotel-casinos became taller and larger, and for the first time, Las Vegas gained a skyline of high-rise towers. In 1980, the effect of the towers increased the density of the Strip. Shut out were the gas stations, motels, and other businesses with small profit margins, which were pushed east, west, and south of the Strip to less-expensive real estate. Parking lots were moved to the back of the hotel-casino complexes, often in attached parking garages.

The denser urban form of the Strip created a more pedestrian-oriented experience than ever before, even if it was an unintentional outcome. For the first time, people were able to abandon their cars and walk between casinos alongside the Strip's roadway. In response to this shift, the Flamingo casino lowered its signage to just above ground level to appeal to pedestrians. The sign's flamingo-inspired light flumes of pink and orange neon were relocated to the building's prominent corner at Flamingo Boulevard and Las Vegas Boulevard South.

A brief recession in the early 1980s slowed Las Vegas' economy for a short period of time, but did not affect plans for new additions and remodeling along the Strip. The renovations continued the 1970s emphasis on larger, flashier porte-cocheres, rather than on casino signage mounted to building façades.

The Mirage, ca. 1990s.
UNLV Library Special Collections.

The Flamingo relocated its signage of eye-catching flamingo feathers closer to street level during the Strip's transformation into a pedestrian environment in the 1980s. Retired portions of the feathered signage are located in The Neon Museum Boneyard. UNLV Library Special Collections.

Some of the iconic symbols of Las Vegas architecture began to disappear in the early 1980s. The Stardust's ground-breaking roadside atomic lettering from 1968 was replaced with plain Helvetica typeface. By the late 1980s, even Fremont Street began to replace its giant neon, façade-covering signs with remodeling transformations to make the buildings themselves more elegant. The Mint's sweeping, hot pink neon sign was demolished when the neighboring Binion's Horseshoe was expanded. The Golden Nugget façade and its historic neon signage were gone by the end of 1986, removed during a remodeling transformation that aimed to make the architecture itself "classier". After the casino was acquired by Steve Wynn, the building lost its collage of neon and bulb signage that spread out across the façade, replaced by a stucco-clad, uniform façade with petite canopies over the windows and doors that were lighted in narrow rows of gold incandescent bulbs. Perhaps most alarmingly, the new façade featured almost no signage and no neon lighting.

In an effort to keep pace with the latest technology, YESCO and other sign design firms adapted to the shifting tastes and began to turn to computer imagery. In 1986, the company acquired its first computerized metal-cutting machine for sign fabrication. The new efficiency brought by the machine allowed the company to make signs faster, and take on even bigger projects that were too large or complicated to create without the aid of computers.

Periods of renewed economic prosperity nationwide in the late 1980s and then again in the mid-1990s led to new waves of construction of casinos and resort hotels in Las Vegas. Newer, more complex hotel towers dominated the Strip and made the older casino architecture appear dated. A new focus on family-oriented tourism brought in a new generation of themed architecture to the Strip. By the 1980s, the importance of signs diminished, replaced by massive pictorial architecture as the new device to attract tourists.

In the late 1980s and early 1990s, the emphasis on themed architecture began to increase along the Strip. The Mirage opened in 1989 for $700 million, taking over the site of the former Castaways motel (ca. 1957) as well as the Red Rooster Club (ca. 1930s). Although the Mirage had a tropical theme on the inside, the architecture and its tall sign did not allude to it, which was a departure from the theatrical exteriors of other casinos that preceded it. The Mirage was designed by architect Joel Bergman as a contemporary skyscraper, with a 3-wing, 30-story glass tower sheathed with 24-caret gold-tinted windows at the top five stories. Characteristically for all of the newest casinos, The Mirage featured none of the neon and lights of the earlier Strip casinos.

1990s

The 1990s represented the final shift in casino-hotel architecture from an emphasis on the porte-cochere to the architecture itself as signage. While this was a distinct departure from the generic towers that were being built in Las Vegas during the 1970s and 1980s, neon and bulbs were still absent in this new trend. The first example of the new building type was the Excalibur, opened in 1990. The building was shaped and themed in the image of a medieval castle composed of a grouping of turrets, fortress walls, and people wearing medieval dress. The Ancient Egyptian-themed Luxor casino followed thereafter in 1991, reproducing

View of the Strip in 1985. Nevada State Museum.

itself required 121 computers to control the moving image at the time it was built. The four-block-long area of Fremont Street was converted into a pedestrian-only street and renamed "The Fremont Street Experience," surrendering the old Glitter Gulch moniker. In 2004, the canopy underwent a $17 million upgrade that included sharper image resolution, and is now capable of 16.7 million color combinations.

The Fremont Street Experience successfully generated renewed interest and business in downtown, and the investment paid off faster than expected. The enormous size and technological sophistication of The Fremont Street Experience canopy attests to the notion that sign design is alive and well in Las Vegas, but vastly changed from its roots in incandescent light bulbs and neon tubing of the earliest generations.

the Great Pyramid of Giza, in a black-glass pyramidal building replete with a sculptural Sphinx guarding its entrance from South Las Vegas Boulevard. Those were followed by New York, New York complete with the Statue of Liberty and Paris with the Eiffel Tower.

The digital age of computers also represented a technological shift in contemporary signage in the 1990s. Signs using LED (light-emitting diode) or LCD (liquid crystal display) began to replace incandescent bulbs and neon tubing. LED and LCD lighting is more energy efficient, using a fraction of the electricity required by traditional lighting and with a longer life.

The displays began to replace the plastic-faced reader boards that had been used for the signs of casinos and small-businesses since the 1950s.

By the early 1990s, the newest casinos on the south end of the Strip had become more popular with

tourists than the older casinos facing Fremont Street. Desperate to generate new interest and dollars in the old downtown casinos, the City of Las Vegas embraced a solution that centered on state-of-the art sign technology. In 1994, YESCO again flexed its design muscles and brought downtown Las Vegas into the next century with its $65 million arched canopy display that stretched four blocks over Fremont Street's old Glitter Gulch. The canopy completely spanned the width of Fremont Street. For a length of one quarter of a mile, the canopy projects a computerized light show emitted from two million individual lights across its concave underside, which becomes a viewing screen when the light show is displayed. Six times each night, the casino signs fronting Fremont Street go dark for a video projected from the bottom of the canopy's ceiling. YESCO's design utilized pixels each capable of producing 65,536 colors as YESCO designers created an innovative light cap that allows each light to be seen from any position underneath the canopy. The video

In August 2007, Glitter Gulch gained another lighting spectacular due east of The Fremont Street Experience, only this time the project returned to Las Vegas' neon roots. The endeavor was the Fremont East District, a three-block stretch created by the City of Las Vegas' Redevelopment Agency and Fremont Street property owners. The project involved streetscape improvements, wider sidewalks, landscaping, and lighting, to bring tourists further east of The Fremont Street Experience canopy. The district's main attraction, however, is the installation of four new 40-foot-tall neon signs that are inspired by historic neon signage. These include a ruby red high-heeled shoe that resembles the Silver Slipper's rotating silver pump and an Atomic-themed "Vegas" sign featuring an angular boomerang and a spiky star for its pinnacle. This recent undertaking pays homage to the glamour and heyday of Las Vegas' Glitter Gulch, and hints at the growing popularity and nostalgia for the city's trademark neon history.

SOUVENIRS GIFTS T-SHIRTS

FLEECE TOPS 9 99
MEN'S GOLF SHIRTS

SWEAT SHIRTS 5 99 2 for $10
JR. TOPS

RTS

ABC

MERMAI

FREE GAS

NAME MUGS
3/10

From left to right, Wayne, Leming, Larsen and Mitchem. *Courtesy of Charles Barnard.*

It was in 1965 that neon sign artists finally got some attention, in one of the essays in writer Tom Wolfe's book *The Kandy-Kolored Tangerine Flake Streamline Baby*. Wolfe pointed out the "designer-sculptor geniuses" who created the Mint, Stardust, Golden Nugget and other brilliant giants. In 1972, in a book more talked about than read, architects Robert Venturi, Denise Scott Brown and Steven Izenour coined the term "decorated shed" to describe Las Vegas buildings which are distinctive because of their signs, not their architecture.

Sign designers had to know art, architecture, engineering and how the elements—neon tubing and incandescent bulbs, for example—work in a sign. The gigantic "spectaculars" had to withstand wind, whether they were freestanding or attached to a building. The sign artists had to be flexible, to respond to the shifting demands of the owners.

The glory days of Young Electric Sign Company coincided with the careers of four designers: Herman Boernge, Kermit Wayne, Jack Larsen, Sr. and Ben Mitchem. Brian Leming, who trained with them and had a prolific career a few years later, called them "The Four Horsemen of the Apocalypse." Between the four of them, working sometimes individually and sometimes as a team, they created most of the iconic signs of that era.

The following seven sign designers are just a few of an important group of very talented artists who created the image of Las Vegas that is known world-wide.

All photos of designers except for Betty Willis, courtesy of Charles Barnard.

Neon Sign Designers

During the heyday of the neon "spectaculars," the 1950s and 1960s, it seemed that the signs designed themselves—so little attention was paid to the artists who created them. Unlike architects, sign designers toiled anonymously. They were valued accordingly by the companies who employed them, usually making less money than the salesmen or even the estimators.

Herman Boernge

Herman Boernge became YESCO's first Las Vegas branch Art Director in 1948. He had moved to Las Vegas after recovering from tuberculosis and went to work at YESCO after opening a free-lance business. His years of commercial art experience as a movie poster artist gave him the grounding he needed to design neon signs. With a flair for both painting and sign design, he created beautiful renderings of the signs he designed: the 1950 open-work Golden Nugget spectacular, the early Las Vegas Club, Mint and Horseshoe; and on the Strip, the Flamingo, the Sands and the Desert Inn.

Boernge collaborated on a sign that was once the face of Las Vegas and still greets visitors to Fremont Street-Vegas Vic. Vegas Vic began in the mid-forties as the creation of a national ad agency, hired by the Chamber of Commerce to promote Las Vegas. Two years later a second agency gave the jaunty cowboy a name and a voice; Vegas Vic's trademark "Howdy Podner" appeared on postcards and newspaper ads throughout the west. The image, officially adopted by the Chamber as its logo, was also used by the Valley Motel and the Nevada Motel. In 1948 Tutor Scherer got the Chamber's permission to use the logo to promote his Pioneer Club with a sign depicting just Vic's head and shoulders, and placed atop a building across the street. In 1951, Vegas Vic received a tall, slim body, and the 40 foot cowboy took his place on the side of the Pioneer Club where he still stands more than half a century later. YESCO's Pat Denner, in Salt Lake City, and Herman Boernge both contributed to the sign design.

Boernge was one of the first sign artist's to fully use three dimensions, for example with his 1949 Las Vegas Club sign, which at 120 feet was one of the tallest of that era. His talents were rewarded over the years with national awards, including two General Electric trophies for sign design excellence. Herman Boernge

died in an automobile accident in 1966. Because of the changing nature of Las Vegas, his legacy of great signs is mostly gone, except for photographs.

Kermit Wayne

Kermit Wayne's designs came from formal training at the Chicago Art Institute, a varied career in commercial arts, and a combination of talent and a way of looking at creative challenges with fresh eyes. After working in Hollywood as a scenic backdrop painter, Wayne came to Las Vegas to work for a billboard company before being hired by Jack Young to work at YESCO.

Wayne's love of a good story usually had a humorous twist. He recalled how, when designing the 1956 Golden Nugget's neon "wraparound" that encased the building in a block-long display, it was discovered too late that the sidewalk had a two-inch rise. The canopy would not have met code at the end where the sidewalk was higher. So he told the fabricators to jack up the end of the canopy, and no one was the wiser! He also told of noon-time excursions with other sign artists to search the local dime stores such as Woolworth's or Wonder World for hardware or even toys that could be re-purposed for sign designs. On one such trip they ended up pawing through a toy bin looking for Roman Centurion figures to use in the scale model of their Caesars Palace design, and having to talk a little boy out of his.

Wayne's other great early project was the original 1958 Stardust spectacular with its space-themed globe. Created the year after the Soviets launched Sputnik, the first satellite to orbit the Earth, Wayne's facade depicted an orbiting spacecraft. The classic space-age lettering was re-used when the huge pylon was built ten years later. Wayne was particularly proud of this design, recalling the fierce competition for the job. "And they picked mine!" he said with a smile.

Kermit Wayne

Jack Larsen, Sr.

Ben Mitchem

Brian K. Leming

Jack Larsen, Sr.

Jack Larsen, Sr. came from a movie poster background, having moved to Salt Lake City to work for a theater chain after spending seven years at Disney. When he came to work at the Las Vegas branch of YESCO, it was not as an artist but in the production facility. Jack Young realized that the company was wasting Larsen's talent, saying to his father Tom Young, "We have one of the best artists in the company working in the shop!" Larsen soon joined Herman Boernge in the Art Department.

One of Larsen's early designs was for the Silver Slipper Casino, a giant high heeled shoe glittering with incandescent bulbs. He used his daughter's dance pump as the model, filling it with cement and of course ruining the shoe. Apparently she was very unhappy about it because it was her favorite pair of shoes. The Silver Slipper sat atop the casino for years, then spent years in the Neon Boneyard. It now lights up the Neon Museum entrance at night from across the street. In another moment of fame, the Slipper can be seen in the 1957 movie "The Amazing Colossal Man" as the movie's hero steps over it on his rampage through Las Vegas.

Larsen collaborated on other projects—among them the Caesars design and the Aladdin pylon. Like many of his colleagues, Larsen was a talented poster artist. He created one of the first airbrush posters on Plexiglas, of Nat "King" Cole. The Larsen name was further associated with neon when Jack's brother Raymond founded Larsen Electric Sign company (now defunct.) Jack Larsen, Jr. worked for Federal Sign in Las Vegas.

Ben Mitchem

Ben Mitchem, the fourth of the great early YESCO design team, created some memorable projects that are still remembered even though they are long gone.

The famous three-dimensional "Sultan" that stood guard over the Dunes entrance as well as in a smaller version on the freeway; the rococo Riviera sign, and a locals favorite, the Leaning Tower of Pizza, also on the Strip. Mitchem was known for his artistic talent, producing beautiful renderings as well as sign designs. He was an important collaborator, though not usually the lead, on a number of major projects.

Brian K. Leming

In 1963 Brian Leming had a choice to make—continue his career as a firefighter or become a full-time neon sign designer. He has jokingly said he made the wrong decision in giving up the good pay and excellent retirement benefits that go with being a firefighter. But his sign artist career was not only fulfilling, it has left a legacy of neon treasures for Las Vegas and the world.

Brian ("Buzz" to friends and colleagues) and his family moved to Las Vegas when he was five. After graduating from Basic High School in 1958, he spent three years in the Navy, joining the fire department on his return. He was approached by a small sign company, Western Neon, and began working part-time as a designer while continuing his firefighter career. At Western he worked alongside Betty Willis, now famous for the 1959 Welcome to Las Vegas sign. After two years Brian made the decision to commit to sign design full time, and left the Fire Department.

In 1964 YESCO purchased Western Neon, and acquired Brian with the deal. At YESCO he worked with "The Four Horsemen of the Apocalypse" as he called them— Boernge, Wayne, Larsen and Mitchem. "They gave me all the little jobs nobody wanted," he laughed. "I was the kid." But he learned a lot, and thrived in the free-wheeling creative environment.

His hard work and talent were rewarded when he was

named YESCO's Las Vegas branch Art Director in 1972. Then in 1981 he and several others left YESCO to form Sign Systems, Inc. (SSI) which completed "more major sign projects than anyone else" during that period. In 1988 the company was purchased by Federal Sign, which was later acquired by Heath, to become Federal Heath. Brian retired from Federal Heath in early 2012.

During his long award-winning career, Brian Leming designed an incredible number of signs, including among others, the Las Vegas Club, the Aladdin Theater marquee, the Westward Ho, Barbary Coast, Coin Castle King, Frontier (porte cochere and façade,) Orleans pylon, the Showboat and the Hacienda Horse and Rider.

Leming commented on the industry's transition from hand-lettered designs incorporating the dazzling colors of neon and the warmth of incandescent bulbs, to today's computer-driven LED reader boards. "They get some amazing effects these days, but the signs don't have the creativity and the personality of the old neon signs."

Brian Leming learned from the great early neon sign artists, but there is no doubt that his achievements landed him in the pantheon of the "greats" himself.

Charles F. Barnard

Chuck Barnard had an early interest in drawing, and after high school studied at Art Center College in Los Angeles. He was drafted in 1948 and recalled to service three years later, leaving the military at the end of the Korean conflict. He married and got a job at a yearbook publishing firm as photographer and layout artist. A few years later he took a position with a commercial sign firm in Stockton, California where he eventually became art director and vice-president.

Barnard began working at AD-ART in 1965, where he was promoted to Executive Art Director, a position he held for twenty years. In 1984 he became a vice-president.

Barnard's many Las Vegas credits include The Mirage pylon sign; "Vegas Vicky" on Fremont Street; the 1974 Stardust façade, the Aladdin porte-cochere and the Union Plaza (now the Plaza,) among many others. He also designed the Reno Arch, the huge sign spectacular for the New Orleans Superdome, and was concept designer for the Stratosphere Tower in Las Vegas.

One of Barnard's greatest and most enduring achievements came in 1993 when he authored a large-format full color book called *The Magic Sign: The Electric Art/Architecture of Las Vegas*. The book chronicles Las Vegas history and the development of the spectacular neon signs that came to identify the town. Included are rare historic photos and sign renderings, biographies of many sign artists, and dazzling full-color photographs of most major signs.

Barnard and his wife Eleanor, also an artist, have four children and several grandchildren. Barnard is retired and now pursues his love for writing.

Betty Whitehead Willis

Betty Whitehead Willis, one of the few women sign designers from the heyday of Las Vegas neon, designed the town's most famous sign--"Welcome to Fabulous Las Vegas." The Welcome sign has remained in place at the south end of the Strip since 1959, even as more opulent creations have been retired. The sign's odd, stretched-diamond shape has made it one of the most recognized images in the world.

Willis was born in 1924 in Overton, Nevada, 60 miles northwest of Las Vegas. Her father, Stephen Whitehead, was the first elected County Assessor. After graduating from Las Vegas high school, Betty attended art school

Charles F. Barnard

Betty Whitehead Willis. Las Vegas News Bureau.

Betty Whitehead Willis. Las Vegas News Bureau.

Betty ended her career at AD-ART, another major sign company, working as an estimator. A single mother, she needed the money. As she commented wryly, "Designers were at the bottom—estimators made more money, and salesmen made the most." She retired at age 77. In addition to the Welcome sign, the Moulin Rouge and the Blue Angel, Betty Willis is credited with the original Riviera pylon, the Normandie Motel, the Del Mar motel, the City Center Motel sign (both in the Neon Museum Boneyard) and the Bow and Arrow Motel sign, which has been restored and is on display on Las Vegas Boulevard just north of Bonanza Road.

Other Designers

Neon artists continued to create stunning designs into the 1990s. The hotels off the Strip built some beautiful classics that fortunately are still standing. The Rio on East Flamingo, the Palace Station on East Sahara, and Boulder Station on Boulder Highway feature three gorgeous neon "spectaculars." Newer hotels such as the Red Rock Casino have opted for a subdued presence without neon's dazzle.

Some of the designers worthy of note include Marge Williams of Federal Sign. One of the very few female designers, Marge Williams created the amazing and colorful Riviera wraparound display. Her background includes a fine arts degree and thirteen years at AD-ART, where she rose to the position of art director at the Los Angeles office.

Lee Klay is known, among many other accomplishments, for designing the 1964 Dunes spectacular. The 180 foot sign remained a show-stopper until Steve Wynn imploded the sign, along with the hotel, on October 27, 1993 to make way for the Bellagio. The Dunes sign won the General Electric Award for "Sign of the Year" in 1964. Klay, who worked successively at Heath, Federal and QRS, had a long career as designer and corporate art director.

in Pasadena. Returning after three years, she held secretarial jobs while moonlighting as a commercial artist. In the late 1940s she went to work at Young Electric Sign Company (YESCO) where she trained with the great names of sign design such as Jack Larsen, Ben Mitchem, and Herman Boernge.

In 1952 Betty went to work at the newly formed Western Neon. While there she designed another landmark sign, the Moulin Rouge. Betty recalls researching French-style lettering in the library to come up with the hand-lettered design. The only racially integrated casino in Las Vegas, the Moulin Rouge Hotel opened and closed in 1955, but its impact lasted far longer. The Moulin Rouge sign is now in

the Neon Museum Boneyard. Another of her signs that is still standing is at the Blue Angel Motel, where a curvaceous blonde haloed angel towers over the motel, a local landmark for many who used to "cruise" Fremont Street in high school.

YESCO purchased Western Neon and with it, the Welcome sign. In 2009 Clark County installed a parking lot in the median south of the sign with room for cars and tour buses. Today it's one of the most popular tourist stops in Las Vegas. In 2009 it was listed on the National Register of Historic Places, one of only a handful of signs so honored. The listing came in time to celebrate both the Welcome sign's fiftieth birthday and the Centennial of Clark County.

Lee Klay.

Bill Clarke designed the 1965 update of the Thunderbird pylon and the new façade with its giant letters spelling out the name. He also designed the glorious pink feather boa Flamingo pylon in 1967. Clarke was AD-ART's first corporate art director, where he hired several talented artists. His Frontier pylon was the world's tallest sign for years. Clarke hired Bob Miller, Paul Miller (no relation,) Charles Barnard and Jack Dubois, putting together a creative team with a lot of synergy and a great deal of talent.

Paul Miller was trained in Industrial Design and started his career with Raymond Loewy Associates in Chicago. He moved to the Bay Area where he ended up being hired on at AD-ART. He only stayed there a few years, but while there he came up with the design for which he is remembered, the 1968 Stardust pylon sign. A stunning cloud of stars rendered in shades of mauve

and blue, the Stardust sign was for many years a favorite of locals, tourists and neon fans. It is now in the Neon Museum Boneyard. The Stardust façade underwent several more remodels, designed first by Charles Barnard, and a later one by Brian Leming. The pylon's space-age lettering was removed and replaced by a plain Helvetica before the sign was finally taken down.

Other artists worthy of note include Heath Sign Company's Raul Rodriguez, designer of the Flamingo Hilton spectacular who was also famous for designing parade floats; YESCO's Dan Edwards who designed the Circus Circus sign with "Lucky" the clown. He also designed the 1978 Sahara super-pylon, at 220 feet, the tallest free-standing sign in the world; Rudy Crisostomo of Federal and later YESCO, who designed the Rio spectacular; Bob Miller of AD-ART, who designed the Bonanza pylon and the three-piered trylon for the International; Jack Dubois of AD-ART who designed the entry arch at the Mirage, porte cochere at the Maxim, and who was part of the team on many other projects, and Harold "Ducky" Bradford, who designed the Buffalo Bill spectacular at Primm. Bradford, who became Art Director at YESCO, had a Master's in Fine Art from Washington State, and a dual career as a fine artist.

Belatedly, these amazing creative artists have been recognized for being pioneers in a field with no formal parameters. They continually broke the mold, achieving artistic triumph after triumph with their own satisfaction usually their greatest reward. Some, like Betty Willis, lived to be nationally known and lauded but without any monetary benefit. As a group, they will never be equaled, especially now that sign design is mostly achieved through computers, and signs are giant LED-lit readerboards. Their legacy remains with the very few vintage signs still standing, and in the Neon Museum's collection.

Bill Clarke.

Paul Miller.

La Concha being cut and loaded. Mel Green.

Paul Revere Williams. Los Angeles Public Library

Paul Revere Williams
Las Vegas and the La Concha Motel

Acclaimed African-American architect Paul Revere Williams (1894-1980) achieved success in a profession which had very few black practitioners. Known for his restraint and elegance, he made a name for himself by designing Colonial and Tudor-revival Hollywood mansions for well-known celebrities such as Frank Sinatra and Desi Arnaz. He also collaborated on a wide range of public and private projects ranging from hotels, restaurants, housing tracts and municipal buildings.

Williams was born in L.A.'s garment district. His parents died when he was four, and he and his older brother were raised by separate foster families. His childhood was a relatively happy one. Williams has stated that he doesn't recall experiencing racism until high school, when he expressed a wish to become an architect. He was soundly discouraged by his teachers.

In 1912 Williams graduated from the famed Polytechnic High School in Los Angeles. He then began methodically making the rounds of architectural firms seeking work. He secured a position with a landscape architect, Wilbur D. Cook, Jr. After that he worked at a number of important Los Angeles architectural firms. At the same time he enrolled in engineering courses at USC.

Williams went to work for architect John C. Austin in 1921 and ended up heading the drafting department with a staff of 20. In 1921 Williams passed the Architecture Licensing Exam and opened his own office, while still working for Austin until 1924. They were later to collaborate on a number of important buildings.

Early on, Williams set the credo that would direct his life. In his July, 1937 essay in *American Magazine*, "I Am

a Negro," Williams stated, "If I allow the fact that I am a Negro to checkmate my will to do, now, I will inevitably form the habit of being defeated."

Williams' talent was fueled by an extraordinary capacity for work. One of his own anecdotes, frequently told in essays and articles, describes how he prepared a design for automobile magnate E. L. Cord in 24 hours, where other architects had asked for three weeks. He got the job. Williams forged ahead of his competition, even with the challenge of being a black man in a nearly all-white profession, by taking on an enormous number of projects and by doing them faster, better and with more value for the dollar.

Williams' handful of Las Vegas projects spanning from the 1940s to the 1960s provides a telling window into Williams' long international career as an award-winning architect. His completed Las Vegas projects included two housing tracts, a horse race park, a hotel, two motels and the Guardian Angel Cathedral on the Las Vegas Strip.

Williams' first project in Las Vegas began in what later became the City of Henderson, just south of Las Vegas, when he designed a housing tract for African-American workers at the Basic Magnesium Incorporated (BMI) defense plant. Called Carver Park, the tract provided simple and affordable homes for hundreds of African-American families who had been recruited from the Deep South to work in the factory making lightweight airplane parts.

The selection of Williams for the Carver Park project was based partly on his having designed one of the first public housing projects in the country, Pueblo del Rio in Los Angeles. He also served from 1933 to 1941 on the Los Angeles Housing Commission, and was appointed in 1933 to the National Board of Municipal Housing. These experiences served him well when he designed Carver Park, which opened in October, 1943.

Williams made good on his concerns for working class blacks when he signed on as the architect for Berkley Square in West Las Vegas. This project addressed the deplorable living conditions on Las Vegas' West Side. After the war, hundreds of blacks stayed on and found other work. Lack of housing, however, was a problem. The 1955 Berkley Square subdivision, now listed on the National Register of Historic Places, provided a turning point in providing decent housing in West Las Vegas.

By that time Williams was also involved in designing a small hotel on the Strip, the Royal Nevada, with California architect John Replogle. (He was also the architect, with Arthur Froehlich, for the short-lived Las Vegas Race Track in the early fifties.) The year the Royal Nevada opened, 1955, was not a not a good one for new hotels, with the Moulin Rouge opening and closing within five months, and the Stardust construction delayed due to the untimely demise of its owner, gambler Tony Cornero, who died at the craps table. In 1958 the Stardust construction was completed and the hotel opened, in the process swallowing up the ill-fated Royal Nevada Hotel for use as the Stardust's convention center.

La Concha Motel

William's next Las Vegas project would prove to be memorable. In 1959 Los Angeles real estate developer M. K. Doumani, purchased a parcel just south of the Riviera with 960 feet of Strip frontage. Doumani and his two sons, Edward and Fred, decided to develop the property themselves. It took two years to secure the financing, hire an architect and build what would become one of the most recognizable and unusual structures on the Strip, the La Concha Motel.

After hiring Paul Revere Williams, Ed Doumani met with him in his Los Angeles office. Doumani described Paul Williams as very well dressed, wearing a three piece suit. The Doumanis explained that they wanted something unusual and eye-catching, but left it up to the architect to decide on the direction and the theme. "I sat across his desk from him while he drew a sketch—backwards and upside down," Doumani has said. The three flowing arches of the conch shell took shape.

The La Concha has been referred to as Googie architecture, a sub-category of Mid-Century Modern which celebrates pop culture and Space-age design with swooping, exuberant lines. Williams was not known for his Googie-style designs, however his later work included several more subdued Mid-Century Modern buildings. The La Concha, something of an anomaly for Williams, still shows his characteristic love of curves and graceful, flowing lines.

The La Concha's engineering is one of a kind, not easily replicated today. The lobby's exterior structure is a web of reinforced steel in the shape of the shell, covered with concrete. The motel section was a more conventional two-story rectangle of 100 rooms, but the whole complex made a memorable impact on tourists driving from Los Angeles with its dramatic façade.

Nevada State Museum.

The La Concha blended high design and hands-on construction, with the two Doumani sons helping to build the interior block walls. Ed Doumani described how, to save money, they shopped at a local hardware store for off-the-shelf dropped light fixtures for the nine bays in the lobby. Yet they spared no expense in other areas. They built a huge, towering neon sign whose base was the distinctive stylized La Concha logo. That sign has been restored and is on display in the Neon Museum Boneyard.

By the year 2000, with the building boom exploding, the Doumani family planned to build a non-gaming luxury residential hotel on the property. At the same time,

In December, 2006, while onlookers from the Neon Museum held their collective breaths, the first cut was made into the concrete-covered spider-web of rebar. Fortunately the building didn't crumble, and the contractor proceeded to slice it into eight pieces. The La Concha Lobby was then moved on flatbed trucks to the site next to the Neon Boneyard. When the Museum, working with the City of Las Vegas, finally obtained enough grant funding, the shell was reassembled in 2008. Ground was broken for the completion of the project in fall, 2011.

Williams designed two more Las Vegas projects, the El Morocco Motel, also for the Doumani family, and the Guardian Angel Cathedral which still stands on the Strip, before he retired from practice in 1973. He designed thousands of important buildings and contributed to many more over his fifty-year career. His career had great value, and even more when considering his struggles as a black man in a mostly white field.

Williams' work is now celebrated at the University of Memphis in Tennessee which has set up a permanent online archive called the Paul R. Williams Project, in partnership with the American Institute for Architects. (www.paulrwilliamsproject.org.)

Ironically, Williams may end up being known for a building that wasn't the most representative of his lifetime of work. The La Concha Motel was a project that Paul R. Williams must have had some fun with, although he may not have thought of as significant. But when millions of people get a chance to see the building restored and functioning as the Neon Museum's Visitors' Center, Paul Williams' name will live on as the man who designed it.

they were reluctant to demolish their legacy, the La Concha. They looked for an appropriate steward for their treasured building. (The hotel was never built; ultimately the family sold the property to another developer.)

The Neon Museum was just then embarking on a major long-term fundraising to build a permanent visitors' center that would lead into its outdoor display of unrestored signs, known as the Neon Boneyard. The Museum had been operating from a borrowed office, with visitation by appointment only. It needed an on-site visitors' center to make the signs available to visitors on a full-time basis.

The project was an ideal marriage of history, architecture and artifact. Historic preservationists, especially fans of Mid-Century Modern, lent their support for saving the La Concha from around the country. Fans of historic Las Vegas neon signs voiced their support from around the world.

In 2005 the Doumani family agreed to donate the building to the Neon Museum. After determining there was no route to transport the 28 foot tall lobby without hitting the freeway overpass, a feasibility study conducted by structural engineer Melvyn Green determined that the building could be successfully cut apart and put back together.

Although the project was risky, it was given the go-ahead. Over the next two years the needed funds were raised, primarily from federal, state and local grants. The City of Las Vegas provided land under a long-term lease for the La Concha. The City had previously received federal funding to build an adjacent "Neon Park" which would provide an attractive and secure block wall fence, to encircle the entire Neon Museum campus of park, Boneyard and Visitors' Center.

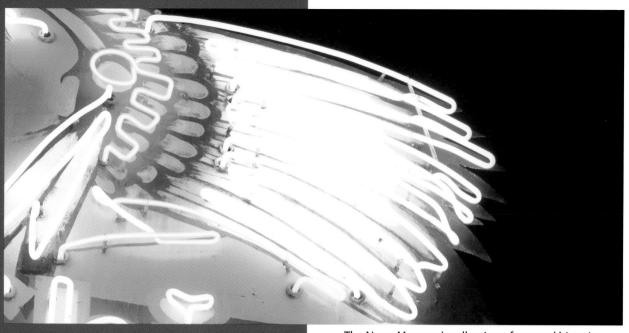

Selected Signs from The Neon Museum collection

As of spring 2013 there were five restored signs on Las Vegas Boulevard North in addition to the Hacienda Horse and Rider at the intersection of Fremont Street. These are Horseshoe, the Silver Slipper, the Bow and Arrow Motel, Society Cleaners, and the Normandie Motel. More restored signs are planned for the median, including those moved from Fremont Street. Signs will eventual extend from Washington Boulevard to Sahara Avenue, the City/County boundary.

In addition to the Wedding Information sign, the Neon Museum has other restored signs in the Boneyard exhibit space. Signs include the lower part of the La Concha Motel sign, and the Horseshoe "H" wall, both of which are next to the Visitors' Center, and a Sahara "S" cabinet. Eventually other signs will be at least partially restored in the Boneyard for an enhanced nighttime experience.

The Neon Museum's collection of rescued historic Las Vegas signs is not just confined to the Neon Boneyard. With the support of individual donors and government agencies (primarily the City of Las Vegas) there are also beautifully restored signs in several locations. Until 2013, Fremont Street had a number of restored signs installed in an outdoor gallery since the 1990s, including the 1966 Aladdin's Lamp, the Flame Restaurant, the Chief Hotel Court, Anderson's Dairy, the Red Barn Bar, Nevada Motel and Dot's Flowers. These signs were removed, to be placed on the median of Las Vegas Boulevard North as part of the Federal Scenic Byways Program. One sign, Wedding Information, is now installed in the Neon Museum Boneyard.

The Neon Museum also has a Living Museum Program. Owners of historic signs whose signs are being used for their businesses are encouraged to participate. In return for being part of the Living Museum, their signs (and businesses) will be publicized on the Neon Museum website. In return, the owners promise to give the Neon Museum the first chance to obtain the sign if the owners need to remove it for any reason. The El Cortez Hotel has agreed to be part of the program and there are several others who have expressed interest. This way the beautiful craftsmanship and the history can be maintained in one place.

The Fifth Street Liquor sign was moved from Neonopolis on Fremont to Casino Center and Garces, near the Downtown Transportation Center. The move was funded by the Regional Transportation Commission. Another RTC project was the Landmark Hotel sign, which is now across the street from the Convention Center on Paradise.

The City of Las Vegas recognizes the value of historic signs. In 2011, the City Council amended the Historic Preservation Ordinance to include signs which are over fifty years old and in their original location.

The Hacienda Horse and Rider

The Hacienda Hotel and Casino opened in 1956, during a period when many new hotels opened, and some, such as the Moulin Rouge and the Royal Nevada, quickly failed. The Hacienda's location at the south end of the Strip proved to be challenging. Owner Warren "Doc" Bayley already owned three motels in California with the Hacienda name. The California Haciendas all featured a similar horse and rider logo, and although they were motels, they provided amenities such as bellhops and room service. Doc Bayley's Las Vegas Hacienda struggled at first until he and his publicity director, Dick Taylor, came up with the idea of handing out coupons in Victorville, California, for a package vacation stay in Las Vegas. Later Bayley began flying customers in to McCarran Airport on a fleet of private airplanes, until the Civil Aeronautics Board shut the operation down as being an unauthorized airline. During the 1960s, YESCO installed the now-famous Horse and Rider sign, designed by a young Brian Leming. Later smaller versions of the sign were placed at the other end of the property and in other locations. Doc Bayley died in 1964 after buying the New Frontier and the Mt. Charleston Lodge. Doc Bayley's widow, Judy, continued to run the Hacienda until her death in 1971. Allen Glick, a California real-estate investor, bought the property and planned a major expansion. After Glick and his partner Lefty Rosenthal were forced out of the state's gaming business, Paul Lowden bought the Hacienda and later sold it the Circus Circus Corporation, later the Mandalay Resort Group.

The Neon Museum acquired the Hacienda sign in the early 1980s. The Horse and Rider was fully restored in 1996, thanks to a donation from Brad Friedmutter, and is currently installed at the intersection of Las Vegas Boulevard and Fremont Street.

The sign was designed by YESCO's Brian "Buzz" Leming in the mid-1970s.

The Aladdin's Lamp (1966)

The "Arabian nights"-themed Aladdin casino-hotel opened on the Strip at 3699 Las Vegas Boulevard in 1966. The YESCO and AD-ART sign design firms had entered into a competition to win the contract for the Aladdin's signage. YESCO won the commission with a concept created by the design team of Boernge, Wayne, Jack Larsen, Mitchem and newcomer Brian Leming, with a contribution by Jack's brother Raymond Larsen. The team's design was a tall, three-sided pylon featuring scrolls that arced skyward and a revolving, lighted, three-dimensional genie's lamp as its crowning pinnacle. Covered in yellow incandescent bulbs on all sides, the genie's lamp created a glowing icon on the Strip for the new Aladdin.

The Flame Restaurant

The Flame Restaurant sign was installed in 1961 on the rooftop of The Flame Restaurant, which was located at 1 Desert Inn Road, Las Vegas. As one of two similar signs created by YESCO, the design is credited to YESCO's Herman Boernge, a lead designer at the company during the 1960s. The Flame, a western-themed steakhouse, was noted to have regularly served Frank Sinatra and the Rat Pack, Peter Faulk, and Betty Grable through the 1960s. The restaurant operated for 33 years until its closing in 1994.

This section of the sign is the top portion of the original The Flame Restaurant signage. It has been fully restored and installed as part of The Neon Museum's exhibit on Fremont Street.

Chief Hotel Court

The Chief Hotel Court opened in 1939 as a motel establishment on 1201 East Fremont Street near the city's downtown district. Its neon sign is believed to date to ca.1940, making it one of the oldest intact neon signs in Las Vegas today. The Chief Hotel Court motel and its sign were designed for the motel's namesake, the Santa Fe Chief and the Atchison, Topeka, and Santa Fe Railroad, as owner Harold J. Stocker and his brother had worked for the railroad company.

The Chief Hotel Court was a classic example of a late 1930s motel in Las Vegas. A motel typically advertised its amenities in text placed on a large, roadside sign, like the Chief Hotel Court signage. The sign often boldly broadcasted air conditioning, a swimming pool, or the motel's proximity to a nearby attraction, such as the Hoover Dam. Stylistically, motels frequently combined symbolic Western motifs with modern materials. By 1941, there were at least 26 motor courts (motels) in Las Vegas, and most of these were located within the city limits along Fifth Street and E Fremont.

The Chief Hotel Court sign has been fully restored, and is installed as part of The Neon Museum's exhibit on Fremont Street.

Anderson Dairy Milkman

Anderson Dairy was founded in 1907 when Las Vegas was still a small railroad stop halfway along the San Pedro, Los Angeles and Salt Lake City Railroad line. Fifty years later, Las Vegas experienced an intense period of growth and expansion during the 1950s. As the population surged, residents established new businesses and neighborhoods to meet the demands of the growing community. The Anderson Dairy, the oldest dairy at that time, followed suit by enlarging its dairy plant. In 1956, Anderson Dairy built a new processing plant in what was believed to be the largest and most state-of-the-art dairy facility in the Southwest region of the United States.

Anderson Dairy commissioned YESCO designer Herman Boernge to design a sign for the new facility. Boernge's scheme was a characteristically polished composition of balanced lettering and an eye-catching image featuring a large, red-and-white bull's-eye cabinet. He adapted a cartoon of the "Andy" Anderson milkman, the company's mascot, into the signage and placed the icon on top. The sign was installed at the new Anderson Dairy plant in a highly visible roof-top display, and remained in place until 1994 when the company again expanded the plant.

The 1956 "Andy" Anderson milkman has been fully restored and will be installed on the Las Vegas Boulevard North median, as part of the Federal Scenic Byways program. The bull's-eye portion of the former signage is housed in The Neon Museum's Boneyard exhibit area.

Wedding Information

Part of Nevada's tourism trade during the 1940s included the attraction of easy weddings and divorces. The wedding and divorce industry became a staple of the Nevada economy as early as 1931 when marriage and divorce laws were more lenient in Nevada than those of neighboring states. Nevada also made itself competitive by reducing its residency requirement when other states reduced theirs. By 1940, wedding laws required no waiting period or medical examinations and the wedding fees were cheap. Businesses catering to the City's growing and lasting market for wedding services opened across the city throughout the decade. Motor courts and wedding chapels eager to attract tourists interested in a quickie wedding posted signs advertising wedding information at the roadside. . The Wedding Information sign is a classic "fishtail" sign that was likely created in the 1940s to draw customers into a motel or a similar establishment.

The Wedding Information sign has been fully restored and is currently installed in The Neon Museum's Boneyard exhibit area.

The Red Barn

The Red Barn originally opened in the 1950s as an antique shop located at 1317 Tropicana Avenue in Las Vegas. In the 1960s, new building owners converted the business into a bar, and in ca. 1962, commissioned YESCO to create its signature red-and-white martini glass sign. The bar was a success, thanks in part to its proximity to the Maryland Parkway and the University of Nevada Las Vegas, and by the end of the 1960s, it had become a popular social center among the city's emerging gay community. When the Red Barn closed in 1988, its owner donated the Red Barn martini sign to the Allied Arts Council and The Neon Museum.

Nevada Motel

When the Nevada Motel opened in 1937, it became the first auto court in Las Vegas to call itself a motel. Located at 5th Street (later Las Vegas Boulevard) and Garces in downtown Las Vegas, the Nevada Motel was part of the commercial strip development along the Los Angeles Highway during the 1930s and 1940s that became the prototype for the Las Vegas Strip.

The Nevada Motel installed this sign in or around 1950. The motel was among a number of hotels and other businesses that adopted the sign's cowboy image from the Las Vegas Chamber of Commerce's promotional cartoon that became the famous "Vegas Vic" character in the early 1950s. The original designer and manufacturer of the Nevada Motel sign are not known.

Dot's Flowers

Dot's Flowers opened in 1949 on Las Vegas Boulevard, catering to the city's burgeoning wedding industry with its "Free Wedding Information" and "Corsages" for couples seeking a quick ceremony on a visit to Las Vegas. The Dot's Flowers sign dates to the shop's opening in 1949, and was created by YESCO.

5th Street Liquor Store

The 5th Street Liquor Store opened at Las Vegas Boulevard South and Garces Street in 1945. At that time, the store was seven blocks from downtown. According to the original shop owner, Gordon Potter, the city's police department considered the store's location to be on the city's fringe, and therefore out of their jurisdiction for patrol. The 5th Street Liquor Store's sign was installed on the storefront one year after it opened, in 1946. Like many other small business owners in the 1940s, Potter designed the concept for the animated neon sign himself and then commissioned YESCO to build it. The sign depicts a three-stage lighted animation of a hand pouring wine from a bottle into a champagne glass, all rendered on a painted metal cabinet overlaid in neon tubing that lights in sequence. The sign remained in place at the 5th Street storefront until the business closed in 1988.

In 2002, The Neon Museum restored the 5th Street Liquor Store sign and installed it in Downtown Las Vegas' Neonopolis exhibit of historic neon signage. It is now located on Casino Center near the Downtown Transportation Center.

Society Cleaners

In September 1946, Society Cleaners opened on East Fremont near 10th Street in the Las Vegas' downtown district. The Society Cleaners sign (pictured) dates to the year the establishment opened. The store operated for over 50 years featuring the same sign until 2006, when the business closed and the store's signage was donated to The Neon Museum collection. The Society Cleaners sign is now restored and located Las Vegas Boulevard North at Interstate 515 interchange, as part of the Federal Scenic Byways Program.

Binion's Horseshoe

Texan Benny Binion created Binion's Hotel and Casino in 1951 when he bought the Eldorado Casino and Apache Hotel at 128 Fremont. In the early 1960s, The Horseshoe began a major remodeling project that replaced the old signs with a new sign spectacular. Binion hired YESCO and their design team of Jack Larsen, Sr. and Ben Mitchem, who collaborated with renowned architects Wayne McAllister and William Wagner. The result was a unified design spectacular that echoed that of the Golden Nugget's ground-breaking, façade-covering signage from 1956, but on a taller, grander scale.

The Horseshoe's new signage featured convex "bullnoses" on each corner of the block-long building, a convex canopy that was swathed in horizontal white neon tubing that covered the building on Fremont Street, and a solid wall of horizontal, turquoise neon tubing that covered the building's Fremont Street façade above the canopy. Binion's claimed their sign was the largest in the world with over 40,000 feet of neon. The sign stayed in place until the property was sold in 2004 and re-opened under the new name, "Binion's." The portions of the sign with the name "Horseshoe" were removed and donated to The Neon Museum, which now houses 17 sections of the Binion's Horseshoe signage.

This portion of the sign has been restored and can be seen at the intersection of Las Vegas Boulevard North and Washington Ave., and is part of the federally-funded Scenic Byways Program.

Blackjack Motel

The Blackjack Motel sign is believed to have been created sometime during the 1950s. The sign originally stood 35 feet over the ground on Fremont Street between Charleston Boulevard and Oakey Street in Las Vegas. It is a classic representation of neon-lighted, roadside motel signage during Las Vegas' booming years in the 1950s. The city underwent an intense period of growth during the decade when the population rose dramatically and commercial and residential development kept pace with the urban growth. As tourism increased, motels like the Blackjack Motel were an outgrowth of an increasing demand for lodging in the city. Playing on Las Vegas' reputation for gambling, the double-sided BlackJack Motel sign is crowned by two illustrated playing cards that are outlined in neon.

The Blackjack Motel sign remained in place until 2006 when the building was demolished, and its sign was donated to The Neon Museum.

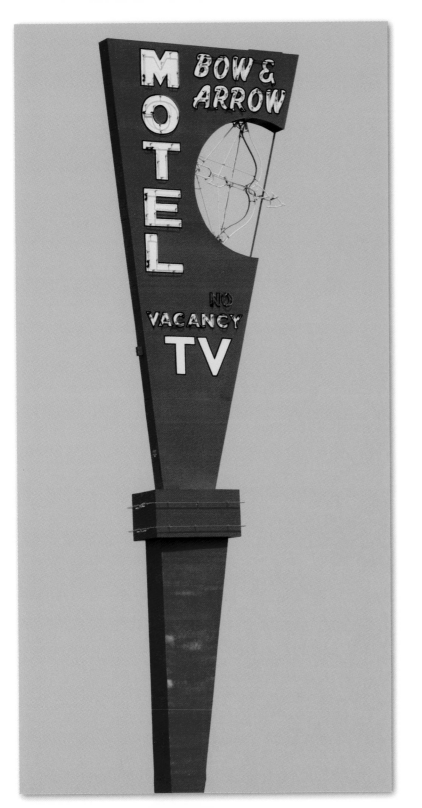

Bow and Arrow Motel

The Bow and Arrow Motel sign is believed to have been designed in the early 1950s by designer, Betty Willis. Willis was among the few female sign designers of distinction during the 1950s. She has earned a place in Las Vegas history as the designer of the city's famous "Welcome to Fabulous Las Vegas" sign, among many other notable and iconic signs in place throughout the city. The Bow and Arrow sign is distinguished by its double-sided animated neon lighting that depicts an arrow being shot from a bow in a three-sequence pattern.

The Allied Arts Council donated the Bow and Arrow Motel sign to The Neon Museum in 2001. It was subsequently restored and displayed in the outdoor, vintage neon exhibit at the Fremont Street Experience area of downtown Las Vegas.

It is now located on Las Vegas Blvd. North of Bonanza, as part of the federal Scenic Byways program.

El Portal Theatre

The El Portal Theatre was the first theater established in the city of Las Vegas. Opening in 1928 on Fremont Street in the city's downtown, the El Portal was the city's first luxury movie palace. The El Portal Theatre was converted into a gift shop in 1978, and the building continues to be used as a gift boutique at its location on Fremont Street. The El Portal Theatre's neon sign was removed around 1994 when Fremont Street was covered by the new Fremont Street Experience canopy. The "El Portal" blade sign currently resides in The Neon Museum boneyard.

The Flamingo

Established in 1947, The Flamingo hotel began as a sophisticated Modern Californian style establishment, in contrast with its Old Western-themed predecessors. As more casinos propagated along the highway south of town, in 1953, The Flamingo was remodeled in what the Las Vegas Sun called "Aztec Modern." The original signs were replaced with larger, more spectacular signage, including the tallest freestanding superpylon sign on the Strip at that time and the 60-foot "Champagne Tower" of bubbling neon lighting.

In 1968, AD-ART's Bill Clarke designed its new super-pylon, which had become the typical type of signage for every major casino on the Strip by that time. Neon tubing was attached to the sign's cabinet to give the appearance of unfolding waves of pink, salmon, and white-colored feathers, establishing the Flamingo's trademark signage at the east side of the Strip.

In 1976, the Hilton Hotel chain bought The Flamingo, and the hotel again underwent renovations with new signage. The new, even more flamboyant feathered signage was created by a new artist on the Las Vegas scene, Raul Rodriguez. Rodriquez had been noted for his award-winning designs for parade floats for the Rose Bowl Parade in Pasadena, California. Heath and Company built Rodriguez's concept for a large, elaborate bouquet of neon-illuminated feathers over The Flamingo's new pedestrian-oriented entrance. The Flamingo continues to use its theme of neon feathered plumes on the Strip. Portions of the retired signage are housed at The Neon Museum boneyard.

The Golden Nugget

Opening in 1946 at the corner of Fremont and Second Streets, the Golden Nugget hotel remodeled its exterior in 1956 with new signage that turned an entire building's façade itself into a sign and thus introduced a new benchmark of sign design in Las Vegas. Rather than using several separate sign pieces along the façade, the new sign covered the entire façade of the old building with what effectively became a new façade itself. YESCO designer Kermit Wayne created the concept of wrapping the building in a three-story sheathing of metal, neon, and bulbs that swept across the building's Fremont and Second street façades from end to end. Although the concept retained the Old Western style and typeface of the casino's old façade, YESCO accomplished the seamless integration of the building and its signage on a larger scale than any other casino had attempted on Fremont Street at the time. Other casinos in Las Vegas quickly copied this unified blend of architecture, theme, and advertisement from that point forward. After years of creating signs that employed only neon, the Golden Nugget's traveling yellow bulbs were also an example of the renewed interest for incandescent lamps in signage in the 1950s.

In 1984, the Golden Nugget removed its signature collage after a change of ownership. Almost all of its original 1956 signage is now housed at The Neon Museum boneyard.

The sign is credited to Betty Willis. The Normandie has been restored and installed on Las Vegas Boulevard's median.

Normandie Motel

The Normandie Motel opened in Las Vegas in 1937 and was located at 708 S. Las Vegas Boulevard on the outskirts of town at that time. The motel installed its pole-mounted sign sometime in the 1940s, where it stayed in place until 2000, making the sign one of the oldest continuously operating motel signs in Las Vegas. The Normandie sign is credited to Betty Willis, either when she was at YESCO or at Western Neon in the early 1950s.

The Stardust

After operating for ten years, in 1968, the Stardust casino-hotel commissioned the AD-ART sign design firm to design the casino's new roadside pylon to replace its original 1958 sign with a much taller 188-foot-tall super-pylon. The new sign featured the letters "Stardust" surrounded by a fuschia cloud with a glittering halo of multicolored, four-point stars that twinkled in sequence from top to bottom in a lighted animation. The Stardust's existing celestial theme and Atomic typeface remained as a continuation of YESCO's 1958 design for the casino. In 1991 the sign's background was changed to purple.

AD-ART's win for the 1968 Stardust commission represented a major coup in the competition for high-profile work in Las Vegas. Staff designer, Paul Miller, won the prestigious General Electric Trophy for the Stardust design's exceptional achievement in electric signage. The new Stardust sign was one of the most popular signs on the Strip among Las Vegas residents and tourists alike for many years.

In 1991, the Stardust replaced its characteristic angular Atomic font with plain Helvetica font. Both sets of letters and the cloud signage are currently housed at The Neon Museum. The Stardust's super-pylon remained in place until 2006, when the Stardust was demolished and its signage was donated to The Neon Museum.

The Silver Slipper

The Silver Slipper casino opened in 1950 on the grounds of the Last Frontier, which was along the early Las Vegas Strip. At that time it was named the Golden Slipper Saloon and Gambling Hall because an establishment named the Silver Slipper already existed in downtown Las Vegas. When the older casino closed, the Golden Slipper changed its name to the Silver Slipper. The new Silver Slipper casino featured a lighted, three-dimensional Silver Slipper that revolved over the casino's building. Jack Larsen, Sr., a senior designer at YESCO in Las Vegas, designed the iconic signage. Like many of the early sign designers of the 1950s and 1960s, Larsen started his artistic career designing theater displays.

Howard Hughes purchased the Silver Slipper Casino in 1968 as part of his acquisition of Las Vegas properties. In 1988 Margaret Elardi, who by then owned the Frontier, bought the Silver Slipper. The casino was demolished and the property turned into a parking lot for the Frontier. Eventually the sign was donated to the Neon Museum where it stayed in the Boneyard for years. In 2009 the Silver Slipper sign was restored and placed in the median of Las Vegas Blvd. across from the Neon Museum. Funding came from the federal Scenic Byways Program, and was administered by the City of Las Vegas.

The Silver Slipper casino was eventually demolished in 1988, and the signage was subsequently donated to The Neon Museum.

It has been restored and is on Las Vegas Boulevard across from the Neon Museum as part of the Scenic By Ways program administered by the City of Las Vegas.

La Concha Motel

The La Concha Motel opened in 1961 at 2955 Las Vegas Boulevard South. The motel building and its curvaceous poured-concrete entrance lobby in the shape of a clam shell were designed by architect Paul Revere Williams. Williams was notable as the first African American architect inducted into the American Institute of Architects, and was honored as an elected Fellow of the organization. His primary office was in Los Angeles, but he completed a number of projects in Las Vegas as well, including the Royal Nevada in 1955 and the Stalcup Shopping Center and Las Vegas Hotel Casino & Shopping Center in 1957.

Designed by YESCO, La Concha's tall street-front signage echoed the motel's aquatic theme by featuring clam-shell silhouettes for the pole-mounted letters and the curvilinear profile of the motel's lobby itself for its base (pictured). That the La Concha Motel extended its theme over from its architecture to its signage reached a level of orchestration rarely realized in non-casino neon signage at that time, even in Las Vegas. In 2005, the La Concha Motel was demolished, with the exception of its clam-shell lobby, which was dismantled and relocated to The Neon Museum boneyard, along with the motel's signage. The lobby was reconstructed in 2012 on The Neon Museum property.

The bottom of the La Concha sign has been restored and is located near the Visitor's Center. The upper portion, minus the letters "E" and "L" is unrestored in the Boneyard.

Standard Wholesale Supply

The Standard Wholesale Supply company began in Las Vegas in 1939 as a wholesale distributor of electrical, plumbing, and waterworks parts to the city's businesses. Originally located at 700 S. Main Street, in 1957 the store relocated to 855 Bonanza Road, which was the main artery into downtown Las Vegas at that time. When the company moved, it commissioned its signature sign that included a double-sided clock and a showgirl swinging on its pendulum. Because sign was positioned at a height to be viewed by passing motorists, its visibility quickly made it a local landmark and many car travelers kept time by the sign's working clock. Former company president Gary Crowe's father established the company in 1939, and had been inspired by a similar sign that he had seen in Wyoming that featured the slogan, "Time to Swing into…" The Standard Wholesale Supply clock's pendulum swung continuously and was subject to strong winds that occasionally caused the time to become slightly off. Apparently, the clock's struggle to keep accurate time on windy days caused quite a stir among people who relied on the clock's time during their commute into the city's downtown area (Crowe, personal communication 2008).

The Standard Wholesale Supply sign remained in place on Bonanza Road for 47 years. When the Hughes Supply company of Florida acquired the Standard Wholesale Company in 2004, Standard Wholesale Supply donated the sign to The Neon Museum (Supply House Times 2004).

Sulinda Inn Motel

The Sulinda Inn Motel was located at 2035 Las Vegas Boulevard (the Strip). According to historical postcards, the Sulinda Inn Motel originally had only a tall pole sign that read "MOTEL" with an angular sign lettered with the name "SULINDA" at its base. At some point, the Sulinda Inn Motel acquired sign cabinets from the adjacent Rancho Anita Motel that were in the shape of a rounded, free-form cabinet and a cactus, which was perched on top. When the signage was transferred to the Sulinda Inn Motel, the larger cabinet was painted from red to pink to match the motel's pink and aqua theme.

All of the Sulinda Inn Motel sign components are housed in The Neon Museum boneyard.

PHOTO COURTESY OF RICHARD AVILA

The Aladdin's Lamp (1976)

The Aladdin's second genie lamp sign was part of the casino-hotel's $60 million renovation and expansion in 1976 that included a new 17-story, high-rise tower. The Aladdin's renovation was typical of the continual remodeling by the casinos on the Strip in direct response to the constant commercial competition for larger and more dazzling casinos during the mid-1970s. The Aladdin's lamp signage was an important and highly visible part of this refurbishment.

The 1976 Aladdin's lamp was designed by YESCO designer Dan Edwards, who is also credited with the well-known sign designs for the Sahara and Circus Circus casino-hotels. The lamp's three-dimensional form was technically difficult to render in metal because of the compound radii required for its rounded shape. The 1976 Aladdin's lamp was removed in 1998 when the Aladdin hotel and resort buildings were demolished.

Lucky Cuss Motel

The Lucky Cuss Motel was located on Fremont Street near the Showboat Hotel, in an area housing a variety of small independently owned motels. As the gateway to Boulder Highway, this stretch of Fremont saw abundant traffic from Arizona visitors. The sign dates from the 1950s or 1960s. The designer is unknown. In 2012 it was installed on Las Vegas Blvd. north of Ogden Ave. as part of the Neon Signs Project sponsored by the City of Las Vegas and the Neon Museum, and funded by the Federal Scenic Byways Program.

City Center Motel

The City Center Motel was located at 700 Fremont Street in downtown Las Vegas. A source indicates that the motel was possibly built in 1957, which suggests that its roadside sign could also date to 1957. Like the Bow and Arrow Motel sign from the same decade, the City Center Motel sign was designed by the preeminent sign designer Betty Willis of Western Neon.

The Green Shack

The Green Shack restaurant operated continuously from the early thirties until its closing in 1999 at 2504 East Fremont Street in Las Vegas. Established as a business catering to the Hoover Dam's construction workers and suppliers, the Green Shack was known for its chicken and steaks and its bootleg whisky during Prohibition. When it closed in 1999, the Green Shack was considered one of the longest operating restaurants in the Las Vegas Valley. The building was listed in the National Register of Historic Places in 1994. This portion of the Green Shack sign was one of the sign components that were originally perched atop the corner of the Green Shack building.

Yucca Motel

The 1950s era Yucca Motel was located at 1727 S. Las Vegas Blvd. near Oakey. The designer is unknown, however its intricately woven neon yucca bloom was an outstanding piece of neon art. The motel was demolished in 2010 and a portion of the sign was saved and taken to the Neon Boneyard.

Steiners Cleaners

Steiners Cleaners was a locals' favorite with its animated white dress shirt moving up and down. The smiling face painted behind the neon shirt gave birth to the nickname "Happy Shirt." For many years located at Maryland Parkway and Tropicana in the Safeway Shopping Center, the sign was saved and moved to the Neon Boneyard.

Bibliography

Ainlay, Thomas, Jr., and Judy Dixon Gabaldon. *Las Vegas: The Fabulous First Century*. Charleston: Arcadia, 2003.

Barell, Barbara. *Legacy of Light: The History of the Young Electric Sign Company*. Salt Lake City, UT: Paragon Press, 1995.

Barnard, Charles F. *Magic Sign: The Eclectic Art/ Architecture of Las Vegas*. Cincinnati: St. Publications, 1993.

Block, Mark P. and Robert Block. *Las Vegas Lights*. Atglen, PA: Schiffer Publishing, 2002.

City of Las Vegas. "Fremont East District, " Available online at www.lasvegasnevada.gov/ Government/7589.htm Accessed July 18, 2008.

Davidson, Len. *Vintage Neon*. Atglen, PA: Schiffer Publishing, Ltd., 1999.

Denton, Sally, and Roger Morris. *The Money and the Power: The Making of Las Vegas and Its Hold on America*. New York: Random House, 2001.

Dumke, Glenn S. "Mission Station to Mining Town: Early Las Vegas," *Pacific Historical Review*. August 1953, pg. 257.

Findlay, John M. *People of Chance: Gambling in American Society from Jamestown to Las Vegas*. New York: Oxford University Press, 1986.

Geary, Kim, Jane P. Kowalewski, and Frank Wright. *Historic Resources of Central Las Vegas*. Vols. 1-3. Nevada State Museum and Historical Society. 1980.

Goldberger, Paul. "A Knockout First Look at Las Vegas," *The New York Times*. New York: NY. April 23, 1978.

Gottdiener, Mark. *The Theming of America: Dreams, Visions, and Commercial Spaces*. Boulder, CO: Westview Press. 1997.

Hess, Alan. *Viva Las Vegas: After-Hours Architecture*. San Francisco: Chronicle Books, 1993.

Knight & Leavitt Associates, Inc. "The Historic Properties Survey Fixed Guideway Project Area of Effect, Clark

Koval, Ana. "Historical Architectural Survey Report for the Las Vegas Beltway, Southern Segment, Las Vegas, Nevada." Prepared for the Nevada Department of Transportation, May 1992.

Las Vegas News Bureau. Photo and Film Archives. Las Vegas, NV, 2008.

Mahar, Lisa. *American Signs: Form and Meaning on Route 66*. New York: The Monacelli Press, 2002.

Miller, Chelsea H. "Neon in Nevada: a Survey of Contemporary and Historic Neon Signs in Nevada," Report Submitted to the Division of Historic Preservation and Archaeology, Carson City, Nevada, 1986.

Moehring, Eugene P. *Resort City in the Sunbelt, Las Vegas 1930-1970*. Reno: University of Nevada Press, 2000.

Moehring, Eugene P. and Michael S. Green. *Las Vegas: A Centennial History*. Reno: University of Nevada Press, 2005.

Ramey, Susan E. "Little Church of the West," National Register of Historic Places, April, 1992.

Ryden Associates. "A Historical Architectural Survey and National Register of Historic Places Eligibility Recommendations for Structures Present Along a One-Mile Corridor between Sahara Boulevard and Charleston Boulevard for the Interstate 15 Study, Las Vegas, Clark County, Nevada; NDOT P364-97-013."

Schwartz, David G. "Ambient Frontiers: The El Rancho Vegas and Hotel Last Frontier-Strip Pioneers." Electronic Journal of Gambling Issues: eGambling [On-line serial] 3. February 2001.

Simich, Jerry L. and Thomas C. Wright. *The Peoples of Las Vegas: One City, Many Faces*. Reno: University of Nevada Press, 2005.

Starr, Tama and Edward Hayman. *Signs and Wonders: The Spectacular Marketing of America*. New York: Doubleday, 1998.

Stern, Rudi. *The New Let There Be Neon*. New York: Harry N. Abrams, 1988.

Swan, Sheila, and Peter Laufer. *Neon Nevada*. Reno: University of Nevada Press, 1994.

University of Nevada, Las Vegas. "Neon Survey: Las Vegas Strip, Sunset to Sahara." 2002.

Venturi, Robert, Steven Izenour, and Denise Scott Brown. *Learning from Las Vegas: The Forgotten Symbolism of Architectural Form*. Cambridge: The MIT Press, 1977.

Webb, Michael. *The Magic of Neon*. Salt Lake City: Peregrine Smith Books, 1984.

Wolfe, Tom. *The Kandy-Kolored Tangerine-Flake Streamline Baby*. New York: Farrar Strauss and Giroux, 1963.

Wright, Frank. *Nevada Yesterdays: Short Looks at Las Vegas History*. Las Vegas: Stephens Press, 2005.

Wright, Dorothy and Angela Moor. "Welcome to Fabulous Las Vegas Sign." National Register of Historic Places, 2009.